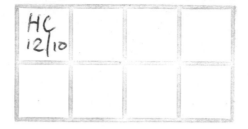

TORN APART

True stories of excluded fathers

Tim Willis

✳ SHORT BOOKS

First published in 2005 by
Short Books
15 Highbury Terrace
London N5 1UP

10 9 8 7 6 5 4 3 2 1

A CIP catalogue record for this book
is available from the British Library.

ISBN 1-904977-30-8

Printed in Great Britain by
Bookmarque, Croydon

Contents

Introduction

Despite this book's subtitle, the truth of the following stories can only ever be partial – and not just because I have edited them, tidying the narrators' grammar and marshalling their stray thoughts. For a start, I have not compared notes with the men's ex-wives or children. Nor have I challenged them on the few occasions that we have differed over the niceties of family law. Finally, I have altered their accounts so that no one can be recognised from them.

Names, locations and – where necessary – professions, direct quotations or telling details have all been changed to equivalents. Thus, Stirling's police have never warned off my 'Ally' character (though another Scottish police force has). Cambridge's housing office never angered my 'Miles' character (though another city's did). If any judges or public servants share the surnames of those mentioned, no resemblance is intended – and so on.

The reasons for this approach are fourfold. First, it is illegal to identify the parties to a British family court hearing. Second, if any children could identify themselves from these accounts, they might be extremely upset, which is not my purpose at all. Third, the narrators' interpretation of the law informs their perceptions, their own 'truths' – so any interventions of mine would be irrelevant. And fourth, if any exes could identify themselves from these stories, they might take revenge on the narrators.

It was such a prospect that dissuaded a judge – yes, a judge – from allowing me to tell his story. He was hurt and baffled by court orders that for several years had denied him regular contact with his children. I offered him the cover of 'a senior civil servant' under which to speak. But for fear of 'disturbing a very delicate situation', he declined. And fear is probably what has stopped such a project as this from being undertaken before: fear of offending all women, who without doubt are the losers in the battle of the sexes. So it's worth stressing here that this book has not been conceived – by its female publishers – in a spirit of misogyny.

We aren't claiming that the narrators' stories are typical of men who have split up with their children's mothers. We aren't waving the flag for any pressure groups, such as Fathers 4 Justice (F4J) or Families Need Fathers (FNF). We don't deny that, of the 50 fathers who cease or lose contact with their children every day, a proportion do so selfishly.

And personally, I'm not even sure that the letter of the current law, which puts the interests of children before parents', needs to be tampered with — although its machinery evidently does.

But the point is, for some time, suffering women have had their platforms. In magazines and broadsheet sections, in *Marie Claire* and on Radio 4's *Woman's Hour*, in pixillated headshots on the television news, one regularly encounters anonymous female witnesses to, and victims of, male cruelty. This book simply attempts to redress the balance. And if it reflects badly on certain mothers, we only ask that you give their accusers the same credence as you might an uncorroborated article on the *Guardian*'s Women's Page.

Indeed, if these aggrieved fathers thought someone was listening, they might spend less time flour-bombing Tony Blair or perching on Buckingham Palace, and more resolving their relationship problems. But then, you can't know what their problems are. Court confidentiality sees to that. And for the same reason, last October, when distraught fathers appeared on Bob Geldof's passionate television documentary attacking family law, they could say how much pain they felt but not how it was being caused. This book gives such men the chance.

Geldof's programme was conceived after statements he made in the media prompted 70 sacks of mail from excluded fathers — more than he got about Live Aid. After reading the first few dozen, he said, he had to give up: it

was just too sad. And I can sympathise with him. In the course of researching this book, I have heard scores of stories whose endings, if true, defy common sense. From those narrators who agreed to publication, I have chosen ten. They represent as wide a range of class, income, location, age, ethnicity and situation as could be surveyed in the time available (and include one grandfather, because the families of excluded fathers also suffer). But some that were left out can't be passed over without mention.

There was Jay. His violent, alcoholic ex – who had been convicted twice for drunk driving with their children in the car – was considered a better primary carer than him. There was Ken. When his estranged wife assaulted him for visiting the old family home – leaving him with blood streaming from his mouth, nose and ears – he was arrested and banned from the street for six months. There was Alex, whose ex was a long-term junkie turned crack dealer. She eluded social services for over a decade by the simple expedient of moving to another cheap hotel in another town. Their daughter went to 26 different schools, and when Alex was finally given (interim) custody of her, she was sleeping on a cushion steeped in urine, in a room smeared with excrement.

The list goes on: Terry had to pay his ex a £35,000 bribe to see their kids; Joe worries his son's step-grandfather is abusing him; Edward's ex-wife has stopped their children dropping in on him, on their walk home from school. But

what happens when these men go to court? Barry had his contact reduced by a judge because it was making his ex – not his son – 'anxious and depressed'. Phil was told he was 'obsessive' in pursuing his rights and should seek medical treatment. Nick was alleged to be 'undermining the mother's influence by providing an alternative home' for his daughter. 'I was only trying to make things nice,' he says. The judge told him to limit his generosity – and when he spent £200 on a Christmas present, he was fined £60.

Every day, the message board on FNF's website is crowded with new complaints. In the lobby of a magistrate's court, one correspondent puts up a poster for this peaceful organisation – which should not be confused with the militant F4J – and is illegally ordered to take it down. A father who has been given two hours every Saturday with his son turns up at the prescribed contact centre on the fifth Saturday of the month – but it doesn't open on the fifth Saturday, and no one has told him. Another gets his day in court, only to have the hearing postponed, because his ex hasn't turned up. There will be no sanction against her and no reimbursement for him – even though she's on legal aid and he's ruining himself on lawyers' fees.

To an excluded father, it might be the final straw. Perhaps he's already worried about his son's schooling. Or he's fretting about what to say to a daughter who he hasn't seen for a couple of years (while the ex whispers, 'Don't worry, darling, mummy will be just outside, in the car').

13

Or perhaps he's a 'bed-sit dad'. I didn't interview any of the latter for this book, because their stories lack drama. But perhaps they are the saddest of all. They may be professionals, they may be unemployed and housed by the council, but their predicaments are the same. The ex keeps the children in the former family home. The dads are unable to have them overnight, because they have no room. Yet the poor worker – in particular – only lives like that because so much of his income goes to the ex, and maybe his lawyer.

Unless a bed-sit dad has supportive people nearby, he faces a soul-sapping, artificial regime, where he sees his children in public places for a day or two a fortnight. He has no legal redress, no battles to recount. All he faces is a long slog – work harder, pay the ex more, inch up the property ladder – and somehow save enough energy for children who are being raised to resent him. Small wonder that, faced with this prospect, some fathers 'give up on the kids'.

Doubtless, it's dangerous to generalise. Every case is individual. But as you'll see from the following pages, various themes about relationships emerge. And one, suspiciously, is that these fathers have done little if no wrong. Now, that doesn't mean they're lying: most back up claims against their exes with sheaves of documentation. But could they be economising with the truth? To be frank, I don't know. I can't check without stirring a hornet's nest. All I can do is give them enough rope to hang themselves. So if you think some of their utterances

reveal them to be unreasonable, judge accordingly.

Certainly, when interviewing these men, I've tried to remember that, despite their suffering, they may still be in the wrong; perhaps their children's interests are being served by the system. The fathers might think they deserve some happiness, too; but they would argue that the law is in the wrong, not them. Dividing parents into 'resident' and 'non-resident', they say, sanctions the estrangement of their children from them and their extended families – which can only be bad for the children.

Many of them believe that, in principle, each parent deserves care of their children for half the time – or rather, that their children would benefit from such an arrangement. The consensus of British psychologists (on which the law is based) disagrees. According to the shrinks, children suffer when they do not have continued and meaningful contact with each parent – but such contact need not be frequent. If the law is to change, the view must change – a vain hope when, as one father put it to me, 'liberal articles of faith state that one parent is as good as two, and that men are abusers and women nurturers.'

So as the law stands, embittered mothers can defy it. Theoretically, they can be imprisoned for doing so (and one or two have, for a few days). But even then, to spite the fathers, they will leave their bewildered children in the care of friends or family – while telling them, 'Daddy told the judge to send me to jail.' Fines, community service, all

these punishments will be laid at the father's door. Thus, judges don't use them – for how can they serve the children's interests? As for the dads, they are left high and dry. Excluded from their own offspring, who they haven't harmed and never would, they frequently fall victims to mental and physical illness.

It doesn't have to be this way. In Sweden, where 'shared parenting' is the norm in such cases, the system encourages co-operation between exes. In some countries and states, the mental condition of estranged children – brainwashed by their mothers against their fathers – has been medically labelled and legally recognised. It's called Parental Alienation Syndrome (PAS) and there is therapeutic treatment that can be ordered for it. But the recognition of this acronym in Britain is no more likely than the reform of two others that cause so much acrimony: the CSA and CAFCASS.

The Child Support Agency (CSA) is notoriously bad at ensuring that non-resident fathers contribute towards the costs of raising their children. But to be fair, it is equally poor at assessing how much fathers should pay, and is unresponsive to requests for dialogue. Perhaps the next wave of reforms can improve it, but the chances seem remote when hundreds of CSA workers are being laid off, while change is delayed at the top.

The problem of the Child and Family Court Advisory and Support Services (CAFCASS) is even knottier. The

officers of this organisation are crucial in family court hearings. Having – theoretically – thoroughly investigated the principals and their relationships, they make recommendations to the judge about future contact arrangements. Yet its own employees will admit the organisation is understaffed and under-trained. And the accounts in this book suggest that too many of its officers are slapdash, opinionated and in thrall to feminist dogma.

Geldof has made some proposals for reforming the British system. He believes in 'shared parenting'. He supports compulsory arbitration before legal wrangling, which is already the norm in publicly funded cases. He thinks that, if action follows, arbiters should file reports to the court (at the expense of their neutrality). He supports better education about the responsibilities of marriage and parenthood – with which I agree. On top of that, I would propose an official inquiry into institutional sexism at CAFCASS, which should be treated just as seriously as racism in the police force. And I believe that there should be a public-information campaign against excluding fathers – as sustained as any in the name of public health – until society's attitudes are changed.

But how about any number of proposals? There's a dining club in Oxford dedicated to overturning the legal precedent of Poel vs Poel (1970). The judgement in this case was that a mother should be allowed to emigrate, despite her ex's objections, because the distress caused by

stopping her would render her less able to care for their children. The anti-Poelites want Britain to copy America, where 'move away' is seldom granted. But in the end, a determined and deceitful mother could still take her child to a battered women's refuge, then a non-Hague Convention country, and the father would never know their whereabouts.

Of course, such behaviour is extreme. At the other end of the selfish-mother spectrum are those who flout court orders in petty ways: they won't pay their share of travel costs to handovers, say; or they want to chop and change arrangements to suit their social lives.

Their exes can live in a state of constant irritation. And one can add to these irritated men all the fathers who are supposedly 'satisfied' with contact arrangements – that is, the 90-plus per cent who reach agreement without involving the family courts – yet seethe quietly at the perceived injustice of their situation.*

It's hard to put numbers on the painful phenomenon of paternal exclusion. The pressure groups say that there are at least 80,000 British fathers whose exes' intransigence prevents any contact with their children. Opponents would claim that a significant proportion of those fathers don't care to see them. And the middle ground is uncountable.

---

* No doubt, an equal number of women feel the same way. As one family lawyer said to me, 'If both sides are grumbling, then you've probably got it about right.'

The courts know that 3000 orders are ignored every year (out of 18,000) but they can only count those cases where the father has the time and means to pursue his rights.

Enough of the general, then. Let us concentrate on the particular. However many excluded fathers there are, and whatever the rights and wrongs, one truth is self-evident from the following accounts. These fathers believe their children have been torn from them – and it has left them feeling torn apart.

April 2005

1. JOCK

'I can still look at myself in the mirror.
I don't know how she can.'

6 October 2004

*It is largely thanks to stunts by the direct-action group Fathers
4 Justice (F4J) that the exclusion of fathers has come to
public attention. However, the group's media manipulation has
rebounded on some of its individual members, whose messy lives and
obsessive natures have provided ammunition for critics.*

*Jock, 48, is one who might fall into that category. Having
children by a teenager, when he was in his thirties, might put him
beyond the pale in some people's opinion. But he undeniably
believes that he is acting in the best interests of his children (Polly,
11, and David, 7). They now live 70 miles away with his ex-wife
Ann, 26, and her new husband, and Jock has them to stay about a
quarter of the time, driving to collect and return them.*

A former miner, when his pit closed, Jock found work as a warehouseman at a local crafts business, rising to become its sales director before being made redundant in 1999. Now he looks thin and ill, with staring eyes that burn in a feverish face. He is a rapid and articulate speaker, jumping from subject to subject, as he tries to explain the web of complications in his case.

He lives on the outskirts of his native Darlington, in a scruffy semi-detached house, where the sitting-room's cheap cabinets are stuffed with toys and games. In one corner stands a desk loaded with legal papers. On the drive sits his rusting K-reg Nissan Micra.

Jock doesn't work and has no savings, so he is spared from paying child support and is eligible for legal aid (as is Ann). Since separating from her in August 2000, he has developed a stress-related back complaint, so he draws incapacity benefit. He cannot afford his rent and leads a spartan existence. However, in return for driving, cooking and doing chores for his disabled parents — who live round the corner — he receives some financial aid.

In this slightly tatty neighbourhood — stranded from others by six-lane roads and suburban superstores — everyone knows each other, and it has been the scene of some of Jock's worst experiences...

***

When Fathers 4 Justice was formed in 2002, the founders decided on a three-year strategy of escalating protest. And although public sympathy was welcome, the main aim was — and still is — to change the law. So if people ask why we

don't try a more softly-softly approach, our answer is: we can't wait! Our children are growing up all the time, and what's lost can never be recovered.

One of my mates held up the traffic on the Clifton suspension bridge, and some people complained that they had lost half a day's work. Well, big deal! He hasn't seen his son for three years. And never mind him — what harm is that doing to the child? That's what we're really trying to do — to give children their rights. They have a right to see their fathers and grandparents, and a whole extended family that can be denied to them. Ann seems to think that she can just dispense with me, and replace me with a new model.

At the moment, I have David and Polly to stay every other weekend and half the holidays, driving a 140-mile round trip to collect them. It adds up to about 100 nights a year. However, for the past four years, I've been fighting for them to live with me full-time — that is, I want to be the 'resident parent' — because Ann's new husband Tony Smith is a violent criminal and he's having a terrible effect on the kids.

Don't get me wrong. My kids have saved my life. Despite the pressure from their mother, they want to be with me as much as possible, and that makes me feel good — knowing that I've got something right. Of course, there are huge problems. David has started using foul language, for example. And he's been bed-wetting and soiling himself for the past couple of years. (That began when I could only see the

kids in a contact centre, with a supervisor present, because a CAFCASS* officer – who has since withdrawn her report – suspected I was sexually abusing Polly.) But despite all the stress, we're happy when we're together. Sunday dinner at my mum's is a family institution.

A bit of me feels guilty that I can't contribute any money to the children's upkeep, but I'm in a Catch-22 situation. If I had a job, I wouldn't be entitled to housing benefit or legal aid. To have any money for lawyers' fees, I'd have to live in a bed-sit – and then Ann could get a court order banning the kids from staying overnight. I've always resolved to tell the truth in this conflict, to play by the courts' rules, and I have. But when I'm being screwed by the system, I don't worry too much if I'm screwing it back. As for Ann, I hate her. I wouldn't care if she were dead.

I blame her solicitors for encouraging her – they're just milking the legal aid system, charging for every libellous letter they write. And I blame Smith's influence – he's despicable. But in the end, I suppose it's her parents' fault. They were starting up a business when she was young, and they didn't have any time for her. She needed affection but when she had any problems, they just threw money at her. It's the same today: they bought her a new car; they bought her a new house when she moved

* Children and Family Court Advisory and Support Service (see Introduction)

23

to Carlisle. Perhaps that's why she liked older men: she needed a father figure. It was never a problem between us, and Smith is about the same age as me.

You'd probably call me a late developer. By the age of 37, I'd only had one big relationship. (Catherine and I were together for two years – living in each other's flats – but sadly, it was not to be.) Ann came from a village near Durham. We met here early in 1993, and we truly fell in love. I gave her time and space to consider whether she wanted a physical relationship, and she entered into it gladly. She fell pregnant almost immediately, and when Polly was born, we all moved into a rented flat in Newcastle, about ten miles the other side of her parents' house. I was working ten-hour days, and moving up the crafts company. She sorted out some childminding and joined an NVQ (National Vocational Qualification) course at a nearby college. Even then, I now realise, I was doing the lion's share of the housework and childcare, but I didn't mind because I was so in love.

A week before Christmas 1994, she announced that she had met a new man at the college and was leaving me. I begged her not to, but the next day she took Polly to her parents'. Eventually, I moved back in with mine. But over the next year, I saw Polly every weekend, and I pursued Ann – even though she'd now started seeing another guy. When she split up with him, she came back to me. And because I loved her, I was happy. We bought a maisonette in

24

Newcastle, got married in 1996, and planned for another child – David – who was born the next year.

After weaning David, Ann took some part-time work, first as a waitress, then for her father's company. Around this time, she also told me something that she had never told anyone else: when she was 13, a man in her village had sexually abused her. I really supported her then. I came with her to tell her parents – but they didn't want to hear it, they didn't want a scandal. I tried to help Ann press charges (though nothing could be proved in the end). And that's what makes me so angry about the part she played in the abuse allegations. Still, I can look at myself in the mirror every morning. I don't know how she can.

Anyway, it was time for a bigger home, and for Polly to start her education. The schools are better here, so we took a mortgage on a three-bedroom house. A fortnight after completing – on Boxing Day 1998 – Ann told me she had been having another affair, with another guy in Newcastle, and was setting up home with him. She took the kids in February, which meant Polly had to change schools, but I still hoped I could get her back. In the meantime, I saw the children every weekend and had them overnight on Wednesdays – a situation that carried on until April 1999, when things went really crazy.

Having split up with boyfriend number three, Ann had fallen pregnant again – by a guy called Joe, who didn't want to know. She wanted a termination and begged for my

support. She said, if I could do that, she could mend her ways. Two days later — even though I told her we were finished if she did it — she went to see Joe again. Two days after that, I had a one-night stand with a friend. The result was that Ann attacked me in front of the kids, kicked my car in, and went round to the house, where she trashed our bedroom and wrote 'Bastard' all over the walls.

The next day she had the termination, and in the evening she called me and asked if I would go over. I said no and put the phone down. A while later, a friend rang to say she was waving a carving knife around and threatening to commit suicide. I was worried about the kids, so I drove round to her place and disarmed her. I spent the night on her settee, and in the morning took her to the doctor's, got her some sedatives and arranged for her friend to keep a special eye on her.

It seems incredible now, but a few weeks later, we patched things up and she moved back in (which meant a third school for Polly). I'm not confrontational, but this time I said things had to be different. I was sick of coming home to find the house in a mess, the breakfast dishes in the sink, David's nappy full to the brim. There would be knives and scissors lying round, dirty plates on the floor, Ann's asthma inhalers in reach — and her lying on the sofa saying she was 'exhausted' from 'caring'. It turned out I needn't have made that speech because, within days, I was made redundant.

After splashing out on a foreign holiday and some home improvements, we decided on a role reversal. I didn't really have enough formal qualifications for a new career at my age – and not only did Ann have higher earning potential than me, she wanted to get out in the world. So I became a house-husband with a part-time job, and Ann found full-time work with the council, who offered her a career path and training. While we were waiting for her salary to rise, money was short, but Ann's father stepped in. He bought the house from us and then rented it back at a reduced rate.

For a few months we were in heaven, a real happy family, but by June there was clearly something wrong. Ann said she wanted to move back to Newcastle, to go out two or three times a week and to stay out all night once a month. And that was when I fell out of love with her. I told her our marriage was over – which was the first time I'd rejected her – and after a few crocodile tears, that's exactly how she behaved.

She started to go out every night, sometimes not returning until the next morning. I had to give up my part-time job to look after the kids. In August, I contacted the local housing department about finding my own property, and a solicitor about a residence order for the children. Like I say, I had decided to be straight in all my dealings, so I told Ann. She attacked me, of course – and then, a few weeks later, she took the kids off to her new man, a few streets away.

(It's legal for a mother to do that; but if a father does the same, he can be charged with abduction.) Over the next couple of days, we agreed a deal on the phone: we would have 'shared residence' until a court decided the matter. But then I discovered she was living with Tony Smith. After taking legal advice, I decided all bets were off.

Ann and I both knew Smith's ex-partner Sandy, so Ann knew his reputation. He has a criminal record stretching back to the Seventies, including burglary, theft, robbery, fraud and various acts of violence and threatening behaviour. The local police domestic violence unit, which has records on him from 1998 to 2003, has brought several successful actions against him. The next time I had the kids over to our house, I phoned Ann and told her I was keeping them; she could see them every other day.

Instead, she turned up at all hours, screaming and shouting. The first week, during one unscheduled arrival, I accidentally caught her fingers in the front door, which was on the chain to stop her forcing her way in while we talked. Two days later, I had a solicitor's letter, claiming she had reported me to the police for assault (which she hadn't, as it happens). A week after that, Ann, Smith and two policemen turned up on my doorstep claiming I was harbouring heroin addicts. Now, I don't even smoke dope – I had given up a few months before, precisely because I anticipated allegations of drug use – and since only the kids were with me, I was happy for them to search the house.

Ah yes, the house. When all this blew up, Ann's parents had said I could carry on as a tenant. They agreed it was the best place for the kids to be, but the next thing I knew, they served an eviction notice. Ann would use that against me in our first hearing in October, an 'interim contact hearing'. As well as requesting a non-molestation order, she said that I would shortly be homeless, and claimed that, if I had a home, I would deny her reasonable contact. She also said that she was so scared of me that she only dared to hand over the kids on 'neutral ground' – and worse, that Polly's head teacher had reported a deterioration in her behaviour.

Luckily, I had a letter from the head teacher to disprove that lie. (Ann hadn't even talked to her.) Plus, the judge refused a non-molestation order, and granted me continued residence, pending a CAFCASS report. Ann could pick up the kids on Saturdays from 10 till 6, and for a couple of hours each on Mondays and Wednesdays, so long as Smith wasn't present at the handovers. Of course, I couldn't stop Ann making up more lies about assault and abusive behaviour – they went on for years – but I was satisfied. It seemed that justice was being done.

That feeling didn't last long. By November, we were back in court, where the moronic judge ordered that we should have shared residence in our house until I found somewhere else to live! Ann was to have four days a week, I was to have three – spending the rest at my parents – and it was like packing for a camping holiday ten times a month.

The changeovers were conducted in complete silence, but on the phone we argued constantly about bills, cleaning, shopping, you name it. Meanwhile, I had the first of two appointments with the CAFCASS officer, a bossy twat called Mrs Hudson. Despite the agency's stated policy of equal opportunities, I later found out that Ann had three.

I told Mrs Hudson my story and that, if I had residence, I'd allow Ann whatever contact the court ordered. I informed her about Smith's record and asked her to confirm it with the police. However, when her report appeared in December, it showed that she had checked up on me but not on Smith. She seemed to have been brainwashed by Ann. Regarding Smith, about all she had to say was that there was 'no evidence that his children [by Sandy] have been physically harmed'. And amazingly, she recommended that Ann be granted residence.

In January 2001, I moved into this place. At the time, my solicitor said not to worry about Mrs Hudson: we would challenge all the inaccuracies at the official 'first residence hearing' in February. But outside court, he changed his tune. Though our barrister asked a couple of half-hearted questions, he just seemed to assume that the judge – who was called Simpson – would find for Ann. And he did. Now, if I ever wanted to see my children, I would have to negotiate with Ann for permission.

The terms agreed were these: four weeks a year during the school holidays; Tuesdays from 4 till 6-30;

and – alternately – Friday afternoon till Saturday morning, and Friday afternoon till Sunday afternoon. The order also stated that, for the first three months, the children couldn't have unsupervised contact with Smith. After that, my solicitor dropped me, and I had to travel 40 miles to find a legal aid guy who would take me on. Still, I pushed through a divorce, on the grounds of unreasonable behaviour – she wouldn't admit to adultery – and at least the contact arrangements were working. That is, until 21 April.

That day is etched in my mind. Sandy had called to say that Smith was harassing her, so I went round to her place with my camera. Soon enough, Ann and Smith drove by with the kids in the back. They were making V-signs and swearing through the windows, so I took a picture. The next I knew, Smith had stormed into the house, head-butted me and tried to grab my camera. Ann pulled him off and hustled him into the car. And as they drove away, I could see my kids in the back window, crying and screaming for me.

As I was soon to discover, they had actually left the area – with Ann telling her solicitor that she had fled in fear of me. Despite a contact order being in place, my lawyer had to hire a private investigator to track her down to Carlisle, tracing her through Polly's school. (At eight years old, she was now on her fourth.) Contact was re-established, though for the next two months, Ann only allowed me the odd day-visit – driving a 140-mile round trip – and completely

denied me my rightful week in the summer half term.

I managed to instigate a court hearing in late June, only to have the proceedings transferred here a fortnight later. When we went to court here, they transferred it back to Carlisle! In the meantime, Ann told her solicitor that she had been advised by David's health visitor to reduce contact, because the travelling was too tiring. I checked that out. It was a lie – but it would be repeated again in court.

Lies, lies and more lies. In the middle of my fortnight with the kids during the summer holidays, Ann told me she needed them back for a special day out with my in-laws, but her parents never turned up. In August, Ann alleged that Smith's son had found some dope in my car when I was visiting Sandy. (It turned out that Smith had put the boy up to it.) There were a couple more court appearances between then and December, and a three-week period when Ann denied contact. But of course, she wasn't penalised – the judges always think the mother's faults are water under the bridge.

During that time, a new CAFCASS report was being compiled, this time by a Mrs Harris. She was even worse than Mrs Hudson. She repeated Ann's allegation that I was coaching the children to say they wanted to come and live with me, but omitted a letter I gave her from Polly's head teacher, which confirmed that Polly had independently told several staff members that was what she wanted. Mrs Harris even recorded Smith's account of events and ignored

mine. And on top of that, she said that my son's bedroom was bland. If you want to look, it's painted lime-green, has his posters on the wall and a Spiderman duvet!

Then came the bombshell. When Mrs Hudson had made a home visit, Polly had sat on my knee to show her a photo album. My hand was round her waist and, apparently, I was rubbing her tummy. Now, that's nothing special with a seven year-old, I didn't even notice I was doing it. But Mrs Hudson reported that it was possible 'grooming'. She also thought the kids' behaviour and speech 'indicated inappropriate levels of knowledge of sexual issues' and rec-ommended further investigation. Too right – and she should have started with Smith.

This was a terrible time to lose my (second) solicitor. Unfortunately, I was passed on to a partner who announced that she 'didn't normally do legal aid work'. Meanwhile, Ann sent a lawyer's letter alleging that Polly had told her: 'Daddy says he's going to put a baby in my tummy.' Naturally, the court ordered a social services' report. But while that was going on, Ann denied me all contact with the kids – apart from five hours, a couple of weeks before Christmas. And at a hearing on 20 December, despite my being exonerated by social services, Judge Simpson ordered that I could only see the kids for two hours a week, under supervision. So that's what I did for the next three months: a 140-mile round trip for two hours a week.

Do you have any idea what contact centres are like?

They're usually in church halls or community centres. To avoid seeing each other, most dads wait inside, most mums drop their kids in the carpark. You're not allowed to take photographs. In the hall, there will be a hamper full of toys and books – half of them damaged – so the kids take something from there, and go into a corner with their dads for however long they've got. Supervised contact is even worse. An elderly woman led us through to a room in the kitchen area, with lino on the floor and nothing on the walls except white gloss paint. There were some low tables in there, and we sat at one, while she sat at another. At first, it was incredibly intimidating. I didn't dare touch my kids. However, once I started taking my mum with me, she got chatting about my case to the supervisor, and the atmosphere improved considerably.

The only other good news in my life was that I found a brilliant legal aid solicitor who worked nearby. But even she couldn't help me get residence. At the next hearing in March 2002, Judge Simpson was only interested in the 'status quo'. He seemed to think that just because the kids had been with Ann and Smith for the last 13 months, it was in their best interests to stay with them. Now, for nine of those months, I'd been blocked by Ann's lies, and the incompetence of the courts and CAFCASS – and for the 16 months before our separation, I had been the house-husband – but none of that mattered to the judge. He ordered a review in September, and in the meantime gave

me back about 100 days a year of contact. I was also allowed telephone contact with each child once a week. But by the end of June, I was too concerned to let matters rest.

By then, both children had told me Smith had smacked them, and that he had twisted David's ear. Also, David had called me a 'little fucking bastard' (why not a big one?) and tried to head-butt me. I began reporting these types of incidents to social services, who raised them with Ann – who, of course, put the blame back on me. One in particular sticks in my mind: a telephone call in September, when I heard Smith shove my son out of the way, after which he was crying uncontrollably. Imagine how I felt, 70 miles away.

Judge Simpson clearly couldn't. In September, he took a few minutes out from a criminal case to tell us that he was 'fed up' with ours. It was only when my barrister threatened to apply for a one-hour listed hearing that he agreed there could be further proceedings in November. He also, thank God, released himself from our case.

Since then, we've had a female judge – they're always better in this type of dispute. And for all her faults, at least she has 'reserved' the case to herself. She's even put a penal notice on Ann, in case Ann denies contact again. Every now and then, she still does – but I would never ask for the notice to be enforced. For a start, the kids would be sent to Ann's parents. Plus, what good would it do them to have their mum sent down? Ann's already told them I want her

in jail. How do I know? Because they've asked me why.

You could say that nothing has changed since then, but all that time, it's been a struggle just to keep standing still. Never mind the lies, the constant lawyers' letters, the contacts denied on ludicrously false grounds. At the time of speaking, we've had seven more court hearings, and in order to keep my claim alive, I've had to accept certain restrictions. In November 2002, I agreed not to apply for residence for one year. The following year, we both agreed not to bring any 'vexatious' residence proceedings for five years. And in between, I've had to endure a hopeless attempt at mediation and a useless investigation by CAMHS.*

The judge advised us in no uncertain terms to attend mediation, and we arranged sessions to coincide with my trips to Carlisle. Between the first and third sessions, I was bombarded with letters from Ann's lawyers referring to these meetings – which were supposed to be confidential. And at the beginning of the third session, Ann announced that she wasn't coming any more. As for CAMHS, they sent a psychologist to interview us all separately in our homes. (Doctor Connolly also watched the kids at home with me – though not with Ann; and he gave an intelligence test to me – though not, so far as

* Child and Mental Health Service

36

I can tell, to Ann.) We all filled in various multiple-choice questionnaires. One of them showed that I was suffering from anxiety – which was too right.

Another residence hearing was scheduled for November 2003, and a few days before, Ann married Smith. Prior to that, she'd always claimed that our legal fight had stopped her, because it took up so much time, so I suppose she thought it might make a better impression on the judge. Then came the hearing. It was scheduled to last three days, but it was over in a morning. Doctor Connolly came to answer questions about his report, and managed to contradict himself several times. In a nutshell, his opinion was that we were both as bad for the kids as each other, so they may as well stay with Ann – and Smith – under the contact arrangements that we now have. The judge followed his recommendations.

My reaction was to join F4J, which I'd read about in the papers. (Result? Ann withdrew contact – and the penal notice was ordered.) Since then, I've begun to feel stronger again, to feel a little bit alive. I've made some really close friendships, and we all support each other. As for women, I've got some good female friends, but I haven't had another relationship since Ann. Polly keeps joking that she'll find me someone, but I always change the subject. The truth is, I can't find the trust inside myself any more – the trust that's needed in a successful relationship.

2. ROBERT

'I borrowed money to pay for a barrister.
If only I hadn't listened to him.'

13 October 2004

*Robert, 58, used to be a successful businessman, on a six-figure
salary in the electronics industry. However, for several years,
his family problems have sapped his earning power. Since the
breakdown of his last marriage in 2002 – and his subsequent
bankruptcy – his income has further declined, from £50,000 to
£15,000 per annum. He has three children – Sam, 18, Joe, 14,
and Rosie, 13 – by his ex-wife Jane, 49. They all live with her, and
he is not allowed to see them unless they request it. He pays Jane
maintenance, but is not eligible for legal aid in any dispute because
of the assets and income of his current partner Eva, 54, whose house
he shares.*

Although Eva is the managing director of a print company in

distant Hampshire, she chose this pretty four-bedroom cottage in Kent so that Robert could be near his children, when Jane lived in the next village. But since Robert was denied contact anyway — and as Jane has now moved north to Cambridge — Eva has exchanged contracts on a sale and they are relocating nearer Eva's work.

Eva has four grown-up offspring. And to complicate matters, Robert has a child from a previous marriage, as does Jane (respectively, Louise, 21, and Keith, 24). Although Robert severed contact from Louise when she was one — with her mother's agreement — his first daughter tracked him down three years ago, and their relationship has since flourished.

It is this experience that sustains Robert's natural optimism. A big, florid-faced, handsome man, with a full head of grey hair, he talks almost warmly about his setbacks. But there are moments when his eyes mist over, and his lips twitch...

***

To understand the psychology behind this mess, you have to know some family history. For example, my mother had a secret affair for many years when I was young; and later, for a few years, she left my father for the other man. Meanwhile, Jane came from an 'exotic' colonial background. Her father had got up to all sorts of tricks, but her mother ruled the roost. I think Jane's mother was protective of her only daughter, and blind to all her faults. The upshot was that both of us had trouble bonding with the opposite sex.

I first met her in the early Eighties, when we were both living in the same Wiltshire village. I was a bit of a flash Harry, a grammar school boy made good. Jane was married, and her Keith was a toddler. We had a four-month affair – which I broke off, because I felt bad about it – and I moved a few miles west.

In the next two years, I met and married Louise's mum, and divorced her. We both agreed we were completely incompatible – I suspect she was having an affair – so I bought her a house and we went our own ways. The trouble was, I had landed a job in Birmingham, she'd refused to come with me, and we couldn't sustain our marriage with me just coming down at weekends.

So now, at weekends, I would drive down to see Louise, who was still a tiny baby. Meanwhile, after having another affair, Jane had divorced her husband, and was selling up their old family home. (I think she was planning to buy a place with her latest lover.) Anyway, I had to pass Jane on my way to see Louise, we hooked up, and one thing led to another…

Jane was – is – a very powerful personality, and soon we were back in a very intense relationship. Unfortunately, she had a problem with my visits to Louise. I guess she was jealous. Anyway, she gave me an ultimatum – it's her or me – and I chose to be pragmatic. Louise's mum was engaged to another man, and I figured a clean break for all of us might be best. Jane and I were married in 1985, when Keith was

five, and we were expecting to move to Birmingham. But then I got a job in Bristol, and we settled in Wiltshire, renting at first.

Almost immediately, I began to feel uncomfortable. Jane seemed to think that we could afford the same lifestyle as her friends, who were all Eton and Oxbridge types, and I didn't want to confront her. Also, she wouldn't let me discipline Keith, and I thought that was sending him a bad message about boundaries. But I was on a roll with my business. And after a string of failures, I was determined to make this relationship work, even if it meant biting my tongue. I put any problems to the back of my mind and hoped that things would work out with the birth of Sam in 1986.

Around then, I started up my own business in Southampton, hiring Eva as a personal assistant. By 1988, with my capital and Jane's, we had a mortgage on a massive house down there, probably worth a million today. I was driving a BMW 5-series, and I bought Jane a 3-series for Christmas. But even though we were living to the limit of my means, Jane kept putting demands on me. She wanted a place with a 100-foot swimming pool, because Keith seemed to have some aptitude, and I agreed. She went off the Pill because she wanted more children, and – well – I'm a human being, you know? And after Joe, she wanted another, which was Rosie. I think she was going to keep having children until she had a girl to replace Louise.

On it went, and every time I was thinking, 'That's another straw.' But Jane had a way of challenging my self-image: 'You'll know what to do,' she would say. 'You'll find a way.' And because I couldn't combat that, I'd cave in. For example, she demanded that, as Keith was at a private day-school, thanks to his father, the other kids had to be. I said we couldn't afford it, and she agreed. But a few days later, she told me she'd enrolled Sam, paid for two terms' fees and I had to honour the cheque. It was the same with the other kids – and eventually, they all went to boarding-school. It was the same with holidays, which had to be spent with her chinless chums in Tuscany. I enjoyed being a dad. I used to rush home for bathtimes and bedtimes (on Jane's orders!). But by the end of 1994, things were coming to a crunch.

I'd been re-mortgaging to fund our lifestyle. And since prices hadn't quite recovered from the property crash three years earlier, I was in negative equity. Plus, I'd got the business into trouble by defaulting on suppliers to pay Jane's bills. In the end, I had to sell a majority share to a backer, and effectively became an employee. Still, Rajeev was a great guy – he paid me six grand a month, so that I could keep up the mortgage and the school fees. And Eva was a rock. She knew the trouble I was in, and tried to keep me on the straight and narrow. She had a fantastic financial head, and I found myself depending on her more and more. After one particularly gruelling day at a trade fair in Earls

Court, I put my arms around her and kissed her. She said, 'I've been waiting five years for that,' and we started an affair that we kept secret for several years.

The next summer, it was Jane's fortieth birthday, and you can imagine the bills I was presented with: champagne, a marquee, a frigging ice sculpture! I didn't pay the mortgage that month, and put some of the expenses through the business, so when Rajeev found out, he fired me – which was fair enough. With no income, we soon had the bailiffs round. And by 1996, the house was repossessed. Jane said she couldn't stand the shame and insisted that we move to the other side of England. She picked Kent because there was a good school here for Joe, who has very bad dyslexia and dyspraxia. So we rented a country mansion, and also took in my widowed mother-in-law. She'd sold her own house in Wiltshire and, while I got a new company up and running, she was paying for everything out of her capital.

By this time, Eva had struck out on her own career path. And though we still saw each other once a week – in motel rooms, carparks, that sort of thing – both of us were clinging to the idea of marriage-for-life. In late 2000, we both decided to talk to our spouses, to see if we could reinvigorate our relationships. Eva told the truth about our affair, but her husband sort of shrugged his shoulders – he was a very distant man. I told Jane that I was unhappy with our situation, and she exploded. She was adamant that she would be moving out after Christmas. I tried to talk to her

43

– to explain how her fantasies could harm the children if they bought into them – but it was no good.

However, the next year, she was still there. Under the influence of Prozac, she had blanked out the whole episode. (She had also blanked out me.) And apart from zero sex life, there was no alteration in her attitude. She wanted the world a certain way – and if that didn't happen, then the world should change. By September, I'd come to a decision. I couldn't leave my children but I couldn't carry on with things as they were. I wanted to make a clean breast of it, so I told Jane about Eva – and she went ballistic, particularly because Eva was older than her. But I said I'd give up Eva for the sake of the marriage if Jane would help make it work. When she agreed, I rang Eva and finished with her. I was unnecessarily brutal, but I didn't want to leave the door open for hope on either side.

In fact, the marriage went from bad to worse. For example, Jane moved Sam to an even more expensive school; at £7000 at term, it cost more than Eton! The only light in my life was the reappearance of Louise – which seemed to annoy Jane. Finally, I said I wanted a divorce, so between winter 2001 and the next spring, while all the other stuff was going on, our solicitors were sorting out the financial arrangement. We agreed that I should pay £1250 a month in maintenance and £850 a month for the children. (I later learned that none of it went towards her rent, which just stacked up in arrears.) Jane wanted everything done

quickly, but my company needed attention. She wouldn't wait while I salvaged the situation by putting it into what's called 'individual voluntary agreement' – and so eventually it went bust and I was declared bankrupt.

In January, I called Eva and we got back together 'officially'. I explained things as gently as I could to the kids – with the older two taking it quite well and the younger two being more confused. Meanwhile, Eva told her husband she was leaving. Then we both came to stay with a friend of mine near here. Eva carried on working in Hampshire, while I set up a consultancy and searched for this house. Since then, I've only seen Joe twice – for around an hour on each occasion – and Sam once. I've had no sight of Rosie, and hardly any sound of her or Sam.

The first time I rang Jane, she said the children didn't want to see me, didn't want to talk to me. Fair enough, I thought, it might take them a while to readjust. But every day it was the same. I emailed the children and texted them; I sent them letters, but only Joe got in touch. For the first week, he was phoning all the time, just wanting to know I was still here. Then Jane put a stop to that by taking the children out of school and on a tour of friends up north. Her friends shielded her from my phone calls, and repeated her line about the children. Another month of this treatment passed before I decided on action.

Now, I couldn't prove that Jane was misrepresenting the kids' views, or turning them against me. I couldn't prove

that, in her anger and pain, she was using them as a weapon against me. And I didn't want to put them in a difficult position by turning up on their doorstep. I wanted the decision taken out of their hands. So, since Jane wouldn't consider mediation, I started the gory court process – usually representing myself because I couldn't afford lawyers' fees. Of course, Jane got legal aid.

In April 2002, I received an email from Rosie, which I suspect was dictated by Sam. It was addressed to me as 'Robert' (which she had never done before), said I'd always been a useless dad, and told me to stop badmouthing Jane, who was the perfect mother. You can imagine how I felt about two sentences, which were blown up in huge type: 'WE WANT NOTHING TO DO WITH YOU!' and 'GET A LIFE!!!' I applied for a contact order – and because I was still trying to stay solvent then – a specific ruling that the children should be put into state schools.

At the first hearing before a magistrate in June, Jane revealed that she had pulled her finger out – as I say, she's a very powerful woman – and she'd got onto a charity that would pay the kids' fees for a couple of years. She also requested that the case be moved to a county court. But when that came round a month later, we were simply asked to consider mediation, pending a review in three months. Sweet as pie, Jane said she would 'happily' enter into it – a promise she later reneged on.

Anyway, we got to the October hearing, and the judge

just ordered a CAFCASS report – the inevitable result being a recommendation to deny me contact. It wasn't the officer's fault particularly – he was following his rule book – but he was unable to see the whole picture. With the kids under Jane's influence, they didn't want to see him on their own, nor with me. On those grounds, he thought they were 'polarised'; and since it would be too upsetting for them to see me, they should just be left alone.

When I received the report in February 2003, I decided to challenge it. It had been a year since I'd seen my children. Now, if the children were so polarised, why had Joe sent me a thank you note for the birthday present I'd posted him the month before? Besides, this guy hadn't considered Parental Alienation Syndrome*. This happens to children when the resident parent turns the children against his or her ex-partner. In several countries it's recognised as a clinical pathology with specific behavioural symptoms – and you could tick every box in the list for my kids!

I borrowed money from Eva to pay for a barrister – but if only I hadn't listened to him. When we went to court a month later, he suggested I formalise the contact I already had, and I agreed. That was a terrible mistake. From then on, the court seemed to think that – under

* See Introduction

an 'interim indirect contact order' – letters and emails were enough for me to be going on with. Meanwhile, the judge ordered another CAFCASS report, which came to no new conclusions.

Amazingly, it took nearly a year to have a review of both reports. Hearings were arranged in August, October and January 2004 but were cancelled at the last moment. (First, the CAFCASS officer took an unannounced holiday; then he rang in sick; then Jane's legal team asked for a postponement the day before.) And in the meantime, there were some developments with the kids. In April, Rosie sent a two-line email to 'Robert', which included the sentence 'Stop contacting me.' But in May, Joe rang several times, to ask if I would visit him at home. Jane agreed, and hovered in the garden while we were in the sitting-room. Unfortunately, a friend of Joe's turned up and had to be shown into a separate room on his own. I could tell Joe was worried about being impolite, so I left before we ever really addressed things. And that was the first time I'd seen any of my children for a year and a half.

Next came a very curious sequence of events. For about a week at the beginning of June, Joe was phoning me all the time from boarding-school. Then he called on Jane's mobile, saying he was in the car with her. He said he was very upset with me, didn't want to talk to me any more and hung up. Three weeks later, he was back on the phone, begging me to come and see him at school. I went the next

evening (which led to the school banning me from its premises at Jane's request). I've never told anyone before what that visit was about. I couldn't even tell the court, because I wanted to protect Joe. But it turned out that he'd been punished for stealing – something he denied – and he dared not tell his mother.

Joe and I had some more contact that autumn as well. I happened to see him when I was driving near his school one day, and sent him a card to say so. He rang and asked me to send him some 'tuck', which I duly did. Unfortunately, the school must have intervened and forwarded it to Jane. She returned it unopened to me. The same happened to his birthday present in December, which I sent to his home. I don't know if Jane ever told him it had arrived. I've got them here, look, still in their Jiffy bags.

Shortly after that, the January hearing was scheduled – the one that Jane's solicitors pulled out of. I think the judge felt sorry for me. He spent two hours going through what I wanted from the hearing and giving me advice on my case. But his main recommendation was that I should throw in the towel. In his opinion, no matter what he ordered, Jane could just ignore it and he would be – in his own words – 'powerless'. And that's true enough. In the course of our proceedings, Jane's barrister had to formally apologise on four separate occasions for her 'inadvertently' misleading the court under oath or in sworn statements, and there wasn't even a hint of a reprimand.

At the beginning of March 2004, I talked to my daughter for a few seconds. Jane put her and Joe on the phone to tell me: 'Stop taking mummy to court.' Still, I eventually got a complete hearing a fortnight later. And after four hours, all I came out with was an amplification of the interim indirect contact order, which Jane had misused when she got Joe's school to ban me. The judge made it clear that Joe was not to be restricted in any way if he wanted to see me, but he ignored my protests about the CAFCASS reports and their author. I still can't understand why. In the hearing, the officer himself said he was unhappy that there was no process for monitoring recommendations; that his own training in the area was a week's session ten years ago; and that as a result, he couldn't be 100 per cent sure of his recommendations' validity. Having trained as a probation officer, he termed himself 'more of a GP than a consultant'.

In summing up, the judge said that he could not give leave for any more reports. He specifically denied me one on parental alienation because there would be 'insufficient resources in the area for the therapeutic intervention required', if the report showed Jane was alienating the children – even though he suggested that was a reasonable assumption! His final remark was that I should walk away and hope my children made contact with me at some time in the future. He then thanked me for my courtesy.

But I couldn't leave it there – particularly when Jane announced she was moving 100 miles north. I wanted to

take the case to the Court of Appeal, applying for leave there in May 2004, and some good came out of it. Three days before the initial hearing, Sam visited me here, no doubt on a fishing trip for his mother. Still, while he was here, he asked me to comment on Jane's version of events. And after an hour, I think he realised that there were two sides to the story – though I've had no indication since.

Of course, the court refused permission to appeal: the judge wasn't concerned how the children came to their opinions, just the result. As for my claim, citing a case in Germany, that the children's alienation was a breach of my – and their – human rights, he dismissed it because the German children were much younger than mine. Yet even adults can be brainwashed – and that is what causes Parental Alienation Syndrome.

I could ask for my appeal to be heard by the House of Lords as a litigant in person, and I assume they would turn me down. Then, the only route left to me would be the European Court. That might take years, by which time the kids would be adults anyway, and I just can't face it. I have to earn money to live, let alone pay maintenance. And I can't let the case – rather than the children – obsess me.

It's not all bad news though. The other day, I was feeling a bit sorry for myself and I emailed Louise. Look at the reply she sent me. 'Don't be soppy, you silly thing. I'm here and your other kids will be fine. Love you very much too, and am really proud to have a dad that stands up so much

for what he believes in. Go for it, Pa!' That kind of thing gives me hope that Sam will come round eventually, and that he might put the other kids straight – though I'd still be upset if they turned against their mother. But that's probably a long way off. Sam texted me this summer, asking me to pay for his car insurance. I replied that I'd consider it, if he gave me a call. I haven't heard anything yet.

3. TERRY

'See this scar on my shoulder? The wife
came at me with a meat cleaver.'

4 November 2004

*Terry, 33, has a room in his family's house in Birmingham. The
property is let to his ailing father — a first-generation Bengali
immigrant from the former East Pakistan — but Terry and various
siblings by his late, white mother cover all the costs. It's a tidy, func-
tional place, apart from one room, decorated in the manner of a
'fairy princess'. This is reserved for Terry's six-year old daughter
Anita, who lives a couple of miles away with her Filipina mother
Pamela, 37. Since January 2002, when her parents first separated,
Anita has only slept at her father's for two nights.*

*Once a skilled engineer in a precision-tools factory, Terry 'down-
shifted' to become a production designer, mainly working in the
heritage sector. Pamela runs her own accountancy business. In the*

financial settlement of their divorce, Terry received £18,000 and agreed to pay £200 a month in child support. His ex-wife's share was worth £150,000. In their disputes over Anita's welfare, Pamela is given legal aid. Unable to afford a lawyer, Terry is a litigant in person.

Just before separating, Terry began an affair with a work colleague, Margaret, now 34. Two months ago, she gave birth to their son Finn, and this new family is in the process of relocating to her native Ireland. Following a court order this week, Terry intends to fly back to Birmingham every fortnight, to have Anita to stay in her room, but he worries about Pamela's intentions.

Although he's a good-looking guy, with shoulder-length black hair and a soft Brummie accent, Terry looks out of condition. He used to follow an impressive fitness regime but, for the last two and a half years, he has devoted all his spare time to legal matters. His complexion is sallow, and he's put on a couple of stone. Still, his eyes retain their athlete's focus. He may claim to have become more sceptical of human nature, but he talks like a winner...

***

It's only as the years have gone by that I've realised how weird my upbringing was. My mum and dad weren't married, and they lived in separate houses – but they had seven children in seven years, with me being the oldest. (My mum also had three older kids by different guys – I don't think she was the full ticket.) My dad – who was only a

54

Muslim in theory – had another seven kids by a woman in Bangladesh. And my mum, who was an atheist, got Christianity when I was ten. I think all that confusion left me with a fantasy of what family life should be like, but with no template to follow. I'm an agnostic myself. Still, ethical and moral considerations have always shaped my life.

Anyway, 1992 sees me buying a nice two-bed flat near here, and I find myself living across the road from my future wife. The first time I saw her, she was cleaning her car. I was 21, and she was 25. It turned out she was the youngest of four sisters, and the last to be living with her widowed mother, who had brought them here when Pamela was 15. They all had homes in the area and, being a very tight-knit, ambitious lot, they were always in and out of each other's kitchens. I accepted that as normal – I thought it was quite good at first – but I had no experience to guide me.

Pamela was qualifying as an accountant, and the other three were all professionals – two civil servants and a dentist – whose marriages to white professionals had given them British nationality. The whole family was very big on churchgoing, but they didn't act like good Catholics. They were very snobbish about Indians and Pakistanis, and they used to call Muslims 'low born'. In fact, they made it clear that someone who worked in a factory, as they saw it, wasn't good enough for Pamela. And fair play to her, she stuck with me. She'd been going out with a doctor

from Colombia before me – he hung around for a while, actually – so I think she was rebelling against her mother, who had been very controlling when she was younger.

Things happened very quickly. I was deeply in love. And, yeah, I was a bit chuffed – you know, dating an older woman got me some respect with my mates. I lost my virginity at 16, and since then, I'd only had one-night stands or the odd two-weeker, but I leapt at the chance of playing happy families.

In the space of one year – 1993 – I got together with Pamela, changed jobs and moved into the new flat that she'd bought. I rented mine out, and shared her mortgage and all the bills – but production doesn't pay like engineering, so I took on a few hours' teaching at night school each week, something I've only recently stopped. I don't regret the career change, though, because this life is much more fulfilling. It also pleased Pamela and her mother. A job in 'heritage production' sounded more prestigious than one in a tool shop.

Their whole family was obsessed with careers and salaries. In early 1994, a Filipino friend of Pamela's got her a job with a charity. She'd soon be earning more, she said, but to climb the ladder – and stay in Britain – she needed a passport. The same friend said he could sort her one out for £700, so I lent it to her, but something went wrong and that was the last we saw of the money.

Soon after that, Pamela announced: 'Terry, I want to be

married.' I'd just come in from work, and it was clear she wanted an answer before bedtime. We talked it over and agreed that our relationship was on a good path, and that this would be the obvious next step (though she vetoed the idea of children until she'd established herself in business, and I went along with that). She wanted a big number for the engagement – we checked into a posh hotel and I went down on one knee with the ring – but the wedding itself was just a family affair, at the local Catholic church.

I suppose the honeymoon was an omen. We'd both agreed on a scuba diving course in Mauritius, but she didn't like the hotel, and she moaned about the facilities. I was having a good time, so I said: 'Look, don't blame me, this was a joint decision.' She didn't like that. And now I think of it, I didn't like her family's attitude to holidays. Once a year, we all had to go with the mother – and the sisters and their husbands – to a villa in Spain or an apartment in Tenerife. And every time, the women would complain until they got upgraded. I thought it was all unnecessary, but I didn't even get support from my brothers-in-law. I guess they looked down on me, too.

When I first moved in with Pamela, I thought she'd stop going round to her mother's so much. When that didn't happen, I imagined things might change with our marriage. But no such luck. Then Pamela's mother died – and you'd have expected, after a reasonable time for mourning, that the women would have got on with their own lives. Instead,

the eldest sister Dori took over the 'head of the family' role. And actually, things got worse.

I was beginning to feel lonely in my marriage. Most nights, when I got home, Pamela was round at one of her sisters'. She didn't seem interested in me. For instance, I've been playing football since I was a kid and until two years ago, I was in a local team – but she didn't come to watch me once in our whole relationship, nor even brought Anita. I decided to train for a marathon, but I already knew her well enough not to tell her. She didn't want me to have a life outside of her control, so I started getting up early, claiming I had a big job on. In the end, she found out and was angry, but I didn't know how else to go about it. And I did it. I've run two London marathons since then.

Anita should have brought us closer together, but it didn't work out that way. Instead, Pamela's twists and turns did my head in, and I still haven't quite resolved things. You see, in 1997, she got pregnant by accident and, even though I was delighted, she was dead set against having the baby. I understood her reasons, and ultimately it was her decision, so I supported her in it. I even went with her to the clinic, when she was six weeks gone – and I've always wondered what would have happened if I hadn't.

When we got there, it was a total nightmare. You know, there were bags of clinical waste lying next to the wheelie-bins outside, and all these doctors and nurses walking around, hugging and laughing. And when we went in, I was

the only man there. All these women sitting round the room, facing this invasive procedure, and I was the only man there. I said to Pam, 'No,' you know, 'this is wrong.' And she agreed – and of course I'm glad – but I can't help asking how she could have put me through all that stress.

She always did like pushing me to the limit. But why, really, did she have the baby? Within a year of the birth, she'd offloaded her onto a childminder, so she could pursue her career. Actually, I remember when Anita was only a few hours old, and I was holding her in my arms, Dori came into the hospital room, grabbed her without asking, and walked off down the corridor. That was another omen. The sisters were going to control my family life – and about the only time I was ever to see Anita was round at their houses, where I was completely frozen out.

I was working like a dog, because once she'd agreed to keep the baby, Pamela took 15 months off. But no one took any notice of my opinions. I worried about the way Anita was given antibiotics whenever she was ill, but Dori just shouted me down. I'd have liked to talk about my concerns to Pamela, but when I got home after night school, she was usually asleep, with the baby in our bed. And it was worse when she got a job – partly because she was setting up a business in her employer's time. When I complained, she said I never told her what I was doing in the evenings. I said that was because she never answered the phone.

To be honest, I was beginning to wonder what I was

there for, what the point was, but I carried on in this awful state until late in 2001, when my friendship with Margaret turned into something more. From her, I've learned how important communication is between partners. With Pamela, maybe I didn't understand that properly. Maybe I was so pissed off, I just gave up.

Anyway, things first came to a head in the May of that year. In April, we'd both sold our flats. Once we'd cleared our debts, Pamela was evens and I had about £8000 profit, which became the deposit on our next place, a three-bedroom house round the corner. We had a six-week gap before we could move in, so we were staying with Dori – and obviously, I was keeping out of the way. Some nights, I'd go to the pub, but I wasn't a boozer. I couldn't have run marathons if I was.

Well, after work one Friday, I went to watch a football game in a pub and had a couple of beers. As soon as I got through Dori's door, Pamela started screaming: 'Terry, you're drunk! I've had enough! Get out, pack your bags, go!' I tried to talk to her but she wouldn't listen. She kept saying, 'You're lying! Just like you did about the marathon!' I went to my dad's and ate humble pie. I was in tears on the phone to her every day – I think she liked to hear me crawling – so after a couple of weeks she let me back, and we resolved to make a fresh start.

Besides, the new house needed doing up. And that's how I spent the next two months, grafting, trying to make it the

perfect nest for our nuclear family. But who was I trying to kid? Nothing in our relationship changed, and in September I got together with Margaret. Of course I wasn't happy about it – I still wonder if I, or we, couldn't have tried harder – and I had a lot of sleepless nights. But in the end, I figured that it would be better for Anita to have two loving parents, who didn't hate each other but had separate lives, than to let the poison in the marriage spread.

In the back of my mind, I guess I wanted to break the news about Margaret gently, over time, so in December I suggested to Pamela that we have a trial separation. She agreed, and I moved in first with a mate round the corner, then in a shared house. Given the way Pamela turned out, I don't regret that. But what I really regret is that we didn't have a watertight deal about Anita before I left. Now, I'd advise any father in my position to sit tight. Whatever the grief, don't leave home until you've got a court order on contact; because once you've lost your resident parent status, you've got to face years of slog and heartbreak.

As it was, she walked all over me – but we'll come to that. During the separation period, we agreed, I could see Anita whenever I wanted. If Pamela and I didn't get back together, I could have her to stay as soon as I'd sorted somewhere proper to live. Although the sisters were always on the scene, that worked okay during January. But in February, all contact was withdrawn after Dori's husband did a Watergate on me. Basically, he's an IT guy, and

61

somehow he got into my room and cloned the hard disc in my laptop. From that, they got access to my personal email, and were able to piece together my affair with Margaret. I think they felt I'd got one over them, and it infuriated them. No one would answer my calls; when I sent emails, I got abuse and threats back; and when I went round to the house, Pamela was never in.

By March, we'd established phone contact again, and I'd talked to Anita, who said she missed me. In April, as arranged, I drove round to our old house with one of my brothers, to pick up some stuff – you know, CDs, books, favourite things. But when the door opened, Dori and the two big sisters were in the hall. They had a video camera, and as far as I can tell, they wanted to wind me up, and then film me when I exploded. They were saying: 'You cunt. You fucking cunt. You'll never see your daughter again. You're a dead man.'

I don't know if Anita was there or not. I stayed cool, and tried to push past them to get to the sitting-room. But at that moment, Pamela ran out of the kitchen. And see this scar on my shoulder? [He tugs his T-shirt to reveal a purple slash about two inches long.] The wife came at me with a meat cleaver! My brother grabbed her arm and made her drop it. Then we got the fuck out – and they were still yelling at us in the drive.

These days, I'd report it to the police – not necessarily to press criminal charges – just to get an incident number

that I could choose to raise later in a family court. I'd do the same if she denied me a visit, too – because the police now recognise emotional abuse as a form of domestic violence – but back then, I didn't know my options: I got patched up at hospital, and negotiations continued with Pamela. Still at this stage, I began to read up on fathers like me, and I hired a solicitor. I had to give him up after I'd spent £1500. I can't say he did me a pennyworth of good.

By May, I was allowed to make one or two home visits. But Pamela wouldn't let me take Anita to my new digs, even though all the other tenants there were together, creative people. In June, I moved again – this time with Margaret – to a much nicer set-up in a warehouse on the canal. It had some shared facilities, but I had a little suite that I could lock, and it was totally safe. (The owner's seven-year old boy lived there with him.) On the day before Anita's fifth birthday, Pamela let me take her there. We had a great time, but you wouldn't have guessed it from Pamela's reaction the next day.

She wouldn't even let me speak to Anita on the phone. Then she sent me texts saying that the new place was dirty and unsafe, and that the smell from the canal had made her nauseous – even though it's quite a yuppie part of Brum. She finished with an email, saying I'd never see Anita again – and in fact it was two months before I was even allowed to speak to her on the phone. Then, Pamela tried to make it sound as unexciting as possible. 'Oh,' she said. 'It's your

dad on the phone.' I've never been tempted to put Anita straight about Pamela, though. I'm just hoping that she'll see through her. She'll see her mum all bitter and twisted, and me all happy and normal.

People can't understand why I put up with so much crap, but I believe in playing a long game. You see, if you run too fast at a brick wall, you'll hit it and bounce off. You'd do better to walk up and push it over, nice and slow. So, my next step was to suggest that I see Anita at a centre – anything to keep the contact going – while I applied for a court order. I did it a couple of times, for a total of four hours in eight weeks. But God, those places are total humiliation.

Still, I got what I wanted. In September, Pamela took it right to the wire – her sisters were even standing outside the court, abusing me as I went in – but she backed down just before the hearing. After all, on legal aid, it wasn't costing her anything, so she could indulge these cases as a luxury. Anyway, the agreement we came to was: I could take Anita out every Saturday, so long as we didn't go to the warehouse; and I could have her for Saturday overnights and for a week and a half of the school holidays, once I had a home which Pamela approved of more.

That was the situation when our divorce went through – which is something else that makes me angry. Proceedings had started in March, when I was still feeling a bit guilty about Margaret – and Pamela seemed to know so much more about the law than me that I kind of buckled. She said

that if I stood up to her, I'd lose all my money and any access to Anita, but if we were amicable and Anita was properly provided for, then the deal I just mentioned would apply. In fact, she took me right in.

It was meant to be an uncontested divorce on the grounds of anonymous adultery, but when her papers arrived, she cited the grounds as unreasonable behaviour and attached a list of ludicrous, unsupported allegations: I was drinking 12 pints a night; all my salary was going on booze; I was a negligent father. The one that still makes me and my mates laugh is that I wanted an 'uptown metropolitan lifestyle'!

Of course, I replied in writing to the court, demolishing all that crap, but it didn't really matter either way: I'd agreed the financial settlement and childcare wasn't an issue. Then I found out what Pamela's promises were really worth. First of all, she put the Child Support Agency on my back, asking for an extra £20 a month. That dispute is still going on, because they can't interfere with financial settlements approved by the courts. Then she treated our contact agreement the same way.

By the end of the month, Anita was saying she had to get back early 'or mum will beat you up'. On the second Saturday in October, Pamela took Anita to Scotland to meet her new boyfriend's parents, only warning me the day before. I was in Ireland with Margaret the next week, so I should have had two days in hand. Instead, the week after,

Pamela changed my Saturday date to the Sunday, then told me 'not to bother', as I would see Anita for two days in the coming half-term. I did, and I also applied for another court hearing, because I could see the way things were going.

At the beginning of November, Pamela took Anita on holiday to Florida. (I'd agreed to skip one weekend; in fact she took two.) Then things settled down for a fortnight – until she received notice of the hearing. I got the normal abuse – 'You're going to lose your fucking daughter' and the like – and on 5 December, at the last minute, Pamela texted, telling me not to come because Anita was ill. I rang the next day and she seemed to have a slight cough, so I said I'd come round at 5 with some presents. After waiting on the doorstep for 15 minutes before they came back from a shopping trip, I was allowed in for half an hour with Anita in her room. But after five minutes, Pamela asked me to leave because she felt 'uncomfortable'.

By the next Saturday, things had calmed down. With the hearing due, Pamela must have realised she had to behave. So Anita and I made Christmas cards in my office, as we had nowhere else to go. The Saturday after, we went to a restaurant for Christmas lunch and arranged to swap presents the next day. But a couple of hours later, Pamela rang me, screaming that Anita was ill on the toilet and what the fuck had I fed her? She also cancelled the Sunday arrangement. 'I'm pulling it,' she said. 'You're not seeing her, you cunt. The shoe's on the other foot now, isn't it? I hope you enjoy

it.' She told me to leave the present in the recycling bin.

I went round the next day anyway, but I had to leave the present with a neighbour. Even though I could hear Anita calling for me, Pamela slammed the door in my face. And even though Anita and I had a great time at my sister's the next week, Pamela managed to spoil it when she came to collect her. She started swearing at me, and made Anita cry.

That became the pattern – always undermining. For example, when I took round Anita's Easter eggs, before a trip to the cinema, Pamela had taken her out for the day. I called the police that time, but they couldn't enforce the court order because there was no one home! It may not sound much, but I was devastated. Ever since, when I go to see Anita, I have low to no expectations: I just can't face the disappointment if I'm really looking forward to a visit and Pamela pulls it. When I do see her, Pamela tries to ruin it afterwards. I think she can't believe I dared leave her. She likes to set the agenda.

Take this place. Because of the warehouse saga, Margaret and I came home to dad's. I applied to the court for the established contact arrangements – which I got – but of course Pamela kicked up, saying it was damp and bad for Anita's chest. It was only when I got a RIBA surveyor and a CAFCASS officer round here this summer that she eventually backed off. Then there was my sister's wedding in Canada this June. Pamela claimed Anita had

67

never met my family and that I might be planning to abduct her. Stupid cow. Luckily, I had photographs from various parties that I could show the court.

You get sussed, you see. Pamela's solicitor kept alleging that I was threatening and abusive at handovers, so I started taking witnesses with me. But you can't cover everything. The worst incident was this September. Margaret has been back in Ireland most of this year, getting ready for the little girl that we've just had over here. I wanted to take Anita there, so she could see where I'd be living, but Pamela wouldn't hand over her passport. After going back to court – for which Pamela 'taxed' me a day's visiting-time – I got my way, and we were due to fly in a fortnight.

Come the morning of departure, and I get a note pushed through my letterbox, saying that Anita has gastroenteritis and can't fly. Pamela had a one-line doctor's note, which she later faxed to me, so I had to abandon the trip. I went to visit Anita the next day, and she didn't seem very ill to me – but it made me realise that I was still powerless to influence her healthcare. The first thing on Monday, I went to the doctor's, to demand that I be informed of any illnesses that Anita might suffer, and I asked to see her notes. They refused, saying they needed the mother's approval, so I applied for a court order. And regarding my contact, I wanted the court to approve my plans to come over from Ireland for an overnight weekend every fortnight, plus a week and a half of the school holidays.

And now, I can say – I think – that I'm more confident. The last month, I've been on tenterhooks, but Pamela hasn't tried anything. And Anita's getting used to her new room.

Four or five months ago, she was booked for an overnight, but in the end, she got spooked and wanted to sleep at her mum's. (Pamela wouldn't let me have her back the next day – nor for three days of the holidays – saying that Anita was wheezing.) Then the baby was born, and Pamela was making obstacles. But the last two weekends have been great. So much of our time, Anita and I never had anywhere to go, except museums and attractions, but now we stay in like a proper family – cooking, cleaning, watching telly. They're the best times I've ever had with her.

The court appearance two days ago made me very chuffed. I was really well prepared by a guy I'd found on the Families Need Fathers website, so I had a statement of what I'd requested at previous hearings, a record of the ways that had been denied, and a statement of what I was requesting now. I was lucky to get the same judge as last time, and he was a bit shocked about what happened over the Irish trip.

Also, I really rattled her solicitor. She fancies herself as a bit of an expert on domestic violence, but I caught her out about the new police guidelines on emotional abuse and she started screaming and shouting, completely lost it! I was calmness personified, and it made a bit of the pain go away after hearing all the crap she has written about me and got away with in front of other judges.

So I start a new life in Ireland the week after next. I've got my court order, I've booked flights on Ryanair for two months — which has cost me about 400 quid — and I'm hoping it'll be worth it. Things looks like they're settling down, but I've got to keep my expectations low. I'm going to check myself on every flight.*

* The next Saturday, Terry was denied contact because Anita was 'ill'. When he asked her how she felt on the phone, she said, 'Fine, I mean, poorly.' Terry reported the matter to the local domestic violence unit, 'who basically laughed in my face'. Four months later, the situation had improved, but Terry was still on tenterhooks. He had made seven successful contact trips, and Pamela had given permission for Anita to visit Ireland for four days. However, in return Pamela expected Terry to rearrange subsequent flights for which he had already paid. At the time of writing, he still has to face negotiations over that. Meanwhile, he has been encountering some resistance from one of his brothers over his fortnightly use of the family home in Birmingham, and is, he says, 'becoming worn out by the whole thing.'

4. ROBIN

'Losing my first son cost me years of torment. Now it's happened again, I've learned how to handle it.'

10 November 2004

If not quite a modern celebrity, Robin, 51, is still a well-known musician. In the Eighties and Nineties, he charted several times, in various guises. Today he concentrates on less commercial projects — sometimes supplementing his income with session work — but only earns a fifth of what he once did. Lanky, stubbly and balding, he's no oil painting, and his naturally hound-dog features are etched with worry lines.

Robin has had two very stressful marriages. The first relation-ship lasted from 1987 to 1992 — though the subsequent divorce took four years' wrangling — and the second from 1999 to 2002. To some extent, their demands reduced his earning power over the years. Lawyers' fees, properties and capital sums for ex-wives,

maintenance and child support payments have also cost him hun-
dreds of thousands of pounds.

For his first son Max, 16, he continues to pay private school fees
(previously £18,000, now £10,000 a year) plus £350 a month
child support. For his second son Luke, 3, he pays about £5000 a
year in nursery fees, plus £1700 a month child support. This has
allowed him a £220,000 mortgage on a two-bedroom flat in
Bloomsbury, which he has just bought for £280,000. Clean, lean
and well stocked, it feels more like a bachelor pad than a home.
However, a glance into the room reserved for Max reveals the half-
lit jumble of clothes, CDs and bedding that denotes a teenager in
frequent residence.

A 'very deep friendship ' with an old flame, Donna, who some-
times helps him with childcare, precludes a sexual relationship with
anyone else. So Robin is resigned to a near-celibate life, where
his pleasures are suborned to the financial needs of Max and Luke.
One son from each marriage, their mothers are Sara, 36, and
Nicky, 37 (who also has a 16 year-old son called Rock, from a pre-
vious relationship.)

***

I've got a theory about women and childbirth. You know
how the sex can go out of a marriage if the father has been
in on the birth? Well, the normal reason given is that he gets
grossed out by seeing a little head emerging from that garden of earthly delights. But I reckon it's because women

can't do it again with someone who has seen them in such a weak and helpless state. In a way, women feel more disempowered by 'new' men than by old-fashioned rotters, and I think that paradox played a part in the failure of both my marriages. But of course there were other major fault lines.

I had a completely normal, loving upbringing in Harrow – though I did go to a boys-only day school. I had no experience of hysterical women or thuggish men. However, both my wives had dreadful families. Sara's mother was a serial shagger who married three times, so I think she was looking for a parent figure. Nicky's abandoned her when she was ten – and Rock's father didn't hang around either – so perhaps she just wanted an easy ride.

Anyway, I met Sara in a Florida nightclub in 1987. She was 20, and on holiday with her mum. I was 33, and doing some recording out there. I was definitely on the pull. I'd been in a relationship with an older woman, Donna, which had broken up after eight years, and I wanted to sow some wild oats. I don't think Sara was a star-fucker – she just had dreams that missed – but she was impressed with me. I, foolishly, was impressed with myself for pulling such a babe.

We fell head over heels in love, and within three months, I'd proposed, she was pregnant and we were living in a huge pad that I had in Regents Park. 'Let's get you used to spending money on clothes,' she said. I should have read

the signs. This was a boarding-school dropout, who'd done a bit of modelling and some extra work in pop promos.

She was incredibly volatile. Any attention on me would make her angry. At first, I blamed it on pregnancy, then breastfeeding (then weaning, then post-natal depression...). If I was driving and we had an argument, she'd try to throw herself out while we were moving. If she was driving, she'd prang the car. And she'd park anywhere. I was getting demands for 20 tickets a week. I was still getting them a year after we split up. Not to mention the cash withdrawals – thousands of pounds from machines. Of course, she denied it, even blaming the cleaning lady. It was only when I was about to call the police that she dropped that story. But she never confessed, because it wasn't – still isn't – in her nature to say sorry. That's how determined some women can be to be right.

So she had Max at 21, and I was there in the birthing room – bonding with him before her, which didn't help – and I suddenly found myself at 34, an older man with a baby and a wife who was out of control. You know, I was fairly right-on, and I didn't know how to handle a party girl. She had no resources. She was like someone out of a movie, and I was cast as a father-figure for her to rebel against.

I don't want to give the impression that I was completely blameless. I was difficult to live with – immature, impatient, irritable, stressed – and I gave her permission to punish me.

But I think she was a borderline-borderline personality. I was always trying to get her to seek treatment. When she refused, I started making up illnesses of my own: my plan was that she'd come with me, and then the doctor could have a look at her. But she couldn't be bothered to get up. I didn't mind her going out with her mates – a marriage has to be based on trust – but she was clubbing four or five nights a week, and I was left home as babysitter, or at least to hire one. And the funny thing is, everything was sorted when she was out. When she was home, it was mayhem.

You could see why. We'd go for Sunday lunch with her mum, dad and step-dad. I'd be sitting there with a two-year-old baby, and her mum would be goading the two men to fight each other. They'd be literally thumping each other over the spuds! Another time, I remember being shocked when her dad offered to pay for Sara's driving lessons and made the cheque out direct to the driving school. 'There's no way I'm writing her a personal one,' he said. And by the end of our marriage, I was the same. If she had bills, I didn't trust her to pay them. I wrote cheques direct to the companies. And I went through her own cheque stubs and credit-card bills, to see what she was spending her money on. She hung out with a trashy set of people and I thought she might have a coke habit that I could help her beat.

You see, I believed in the idea of marriage for life, despite the infidelities. In 1991, she had to admit to one,

when an ex-friend threatened to grass her up. But even when she had a miscarriage, which I know wasn't my baby, she denied it was anyone else's. In fact, I still got shit for not being supportive.

After that, I started some detective work, checking her diary, matching up late-night withdrawals from Soho cash machines. I started phoning round our friends, pretending I knew something, and they all spilled the beans. I don't know how many men she'd been with – I stopped looking after five – but she never confessed to any of them. Instead, she called me a sex maniac.(I'd been desperate for sex and she'd kept refusing me.) I slapped her round the head for that. It's the only time I've ever hit a woman.

Even then, I thought we could work it out. You know, I couldn't bear losing someone to whom I'd committed 100 per cent. In my mind, I gave us a month to talk it through – but nothing changed. There were strange phone calls in the middle of the night. I'd find match books from night-clubs lying around. There'd be long calls to unknown numbers on her mobile bill. I didn't feel angry now, more afraid, but I knew I shouldn't move out until I had a solution. And I knew that the best thing I could do for Max was to look after myself, because Sara was in no fit state to look after anyone. I spent the next year thinking about it. I was sleeping in the laundry-room.

First, there was my work. Even though I was doing very well at the time, I was willing to stop touring, to be on hand

for Max. But to become a single parent, a house-husband with no time for anything? No way. I loved my work, we needed the money, and we'd need even more if we were splitting up. Also, it would be perverse for Sara to be unemployed as well – which is what would have happened – and she did love Max. So I figured, if I left, she might get it together. Of course, they'd always be late for school, and she'd forget to buy his dinner, but I reckoned she'd find a man and they would manage.

Besides, I do believe in the natural maternal instinct – and so do the courts. If I'd wanted residency and she'd wanted a fight, I'd have needed to prove she was an unfit mother, and I couldn't do that to Max. On the other hand, I wasn't going to leave them in the house and end up in a studio flat where I couldn't have him to stay. I decided we'd have two two-bedroom flats in the same street. I'd see Max all the time, and I'd have him overnight on Wednesdays and the weekends. I sold the flat, bought two more in Primrose Hill, and presented it as a fait accompli.

I wish. The divorce was at huge expense to my wallet and my sanity. It wasn't so much the contact arrangements: by battling through Sara's hostility, I had de facto joint residency, and the courts like to keep the status quo. But the financial arrangements were a nightmare. Thanks to her crooked lawyer, we spent the next four years haggling over them. Later, there was a difficult time, when Sara moved abroad. So we're only really sorting Max out

now. Poor Max, he's always suffered.

So where do I start with the finances? I'd put £120,000 into Sara's flat, and I was paying her £40,000 mortgage. (I had a £120,000 mortgage on my flat.) I paid for its decoration, and her car and insurance. I was paying Max's private school fees of about £6000 a year, and giving her £10,000 a year in maintenance. And because of the maintenance, I was paying her solicitor's fees on top of my own. The same happened with my second wife. Because of my generosity, they were both too rich for legal aid!

Meanwhile, Sara's lawyer was convinced I had even more money stashed away. (It later turned out that he was also working on a percentage from her.) He made me fill out forms declaring my assets five times. Once, he threatened not to pass Sara any messages until I settled a £3000 bill that I was querying. And in court, he took me to the cleaners. He managed to claim another £40,000 of my capital, so I had to arrange a schedule with Sara. Taking into account maintenance, child support, school fees and repayment of capital – if she didn't marry – I'd be paying her £38,000 a year for five years, then £30,000 for the next five, and £16,000 thereafter. I managed to do a deal on it with her next husband, a dodgy millionaire called Ian, but that's another story.

During much of that time, I was in Families Need Fathers hell – waiting four hours on Sara's doorstep, sitting in the car to watch Max's bedroom light go off, having

half-terms fucked up, every date rearranged and every contact made difficult. Sara's behaviour drove me to drink, but she was more unbalanced than malicious. You know, we'd be handing over and she'd say, 'Where's my fucking cheque?' Or she'd slam the door in my face. When Sara's boyfriend first moved in with them, Max claimed Ian had hit him. I think, in his own way, he was just trying to get Sara and me back together. But he had to give up on that in the late Nineties, when we both married new people – and his mum announced that they were moving to Greece in the millennium.

By then, I'd been on my own for five years, looking after Max half the time, and drinking too much. The next five years were to be full of ups and downs with him and Sara. (Having moved to Greece, they returned a year or so later, and Max went into a day-school.) But I'll come back to that situation – because I was about to get into an even deeper mess with Nicky. That was one reason I didn't crack up over Sara's emigration: it wouldn't have been good for Max to be around the maelstrom I now found myself in. Also, Greece wasn't too far for weekend breaks, and Max would still be in Britain for term times.

Actually, Max's education became a major issue when I met Nicky. Quite apart from his fees being part of the deal I'd made with Sara, I thought the school was a safe haven for Max, away from his mother. But Nicky really resented it, because her son Rock was in the state system. During the

whole time I knew her, I was usually strapped for cash, thanks to a property deal that went pear-shaped. (I was paying £1000 a month mortgage, ultimately for nothing.) When I was frantic about money, she'd say I should take Max out of private education. When I was simply anxious, she'd say that I should pay for Rock to go to boarding-school as well.

We met when I'd been out of my shell for about a year. Before that, I'd been a date from hell. I was unable to hold a conversation without railing against women and the bias of the courts. Now Max was older, I didn't need to be available round the clock for him, so I could relax, and get my shit together. I went out on the road again, and started to earn some much-needed money.

Nicky came to a backstage party, and she was outrageous. A colourful dresser, a great dancer, an extrovert, she was all the things I wasn't. And although the age gap was the same, she didn't seem as immature as Sara, because she was a mum. (Indeed, I had been partly attracted to her because she was a single parent with a useless ex, so I thought she would understand my problems.) Plus, our boys got on very well, which encouraged my fantasies of a ready-made, cosy, two-kid family. I really felt: 'If I can pull this off, then the last one will have been worth it.' But I hadn't reckoned on her agenda.

Once, she'd made a fair bit of money in a teen band, but she'd blown it. She had a flat and a mortgage, but since she

survived on income support, Rock had been given a pretty rackety upbringing. Now he was also bigger, she wanted to pursue a solo career – through me, as it transpired. She was talented, and with dedication, she could have achieved something. But she wanted to 'do a Yoko', to devour me, to have my life. During our marriage, I paid for her to put on a private concert for various industry people. My mates and I did all the backing and production. Then, without telling me – which was weird – she lifted her guest list from my address book.

Actually, she got weird as soon as we lived together. (Yes, I fell head over heels again.) I sold my two-bed flat and bought a bigger place in a cheaper part of town, so that Rock could sleep over – and Nicky certainly seemed sympathetic at first. She'd even look after Max when I was busy. However, things changed when she sold her flat. Once she'd moved into my room, and permanently installed Rock in his, she had her eye on Max's. 'He's only here six weeks a year,' she'd say, 'and I need a place to work.' She couldn't comprehend how much that room mattered for Max's stability.

I felt she was trying to control me. It was as if she wanted me to blank out my history and become a 'good' version of the partner who'd left her. If I took Max to the pictures, she wanted to know why I didn't do the same with Rock the next week. And she tried to bully me about my tactics with Sara (which, as I say, I'll come back to). When you're

a 'contact parent', I explained, you can't have complete control. 'If you can't have control,' she replied, 'why not give up? It never harmed me.'

Now it happened to be a year when I received some hefty royalty cheques that had been blocked for decades, and she must have imagined I always earned as much. So she called me mean. She wasn't interested in the problems with my other property. And it never occurred to her that I was paying out everything for her and Rock! Later, I even bought some songs from her. Only after the divorce did I discover she'd then sold them to someone else.

There was an all-or-nothing streak about her. A record label actually put up a few grand for her to work on some demos, and most people in her position would have been delighted. Not Nicky. If they weren't signing her for a six-figure sum, she wasn't interested. But I'm getting ahead of myself. First, I got her pregnant and we married in 2000. Then, to solve the problem of Rock's education, I suggested we sell up again and move to Harrow, where I knew the state schools were good. We bought a five-bedroom house there, with her paying a quarter of the deposit and me paying the rest, plus the mortgage. And while I put the builders in, I rented a four-bedroom place nearby. This time, we shared a study, until Luke was born – and things really started to go wrong.

Generally, I'm not sure Nicky knows her motives for anything. I prefer to blame her behaviour on drug-induced

nuttiness. But I know I made things worse when Luke was born. Quite apart from being in at the birth – again – I caused a huge misunderstanding. I said that, although I loved Luke, I could never have the same visceral connection that I had with Max. I meant that I could feel more secure with Nicky than I had with Sara – I wouldn't worry about Luke when I was away, the way I did over Max – but she took it to mean that I didn't care as much.

Pretty soon, we were in meltdown. We'd planned to have children, but not for two or three years: once the builders were out of the big house, we were settled, and I'd extricated myself from my other property. Instead, I was working flat out, and Nicky was in a nightmare of sore nipples and baby vomit. She went off sex. I tried to help. I used to cup her breasts in frozen white cabbage leaves, which works miracles when they hurt. But with the sleepless nights, and all the other stresses, we both became depressed and angry at each other. At least, that's what I think. She wasn't having any of it. As far as she was concerned – and she told me so repeatedly, at high volume – she'd done nothing wrong, and everything was my fault.

When I first suggested Relate, she refused to consider it. In her eyes, you have to be 100 per cent right, you never ask for help. It took until October 2001 for her to come with me and see a counsellor, but then she treated the proceedings with contempt. She walked out of the fourth session and never went back. A month later, she announced that

our marriage was over. I said, 'If this falls apart, we're both fucked. Let me put the career on hold, and we can work on this. Give me six months. By then, the new house will be finished.' She said, 'Sell it now. If you don't put it on the market now, I'll take you to the cleaners.' I asked if she'd met another bloke – she'd been spending a lot of time with Martin, a producer we both knew, who lived nearby – but she denied it.

Of course, I suggested Relate again. But to her, things were either black or white, so exploring grey areas was pointless. If something wasn't quite right, you destroyed it. To her, I was no longer useful except as a source of money – so God knows why she involved lawyers.

At the beginning of 2002, the plan was to do things in an orderly fashion. We'd sell the big house and split the capital 3:1 in her favour – although the opposite had applied when we bought it. That would give her a £230,000 deposit on a £350,000 house, which I helped her choose, just down the street from Martin. I'd get about £75,000 – most of which went into this place, after I'd been renting near here for 18 months.

In addition, we provisionally agreed that I would take Luke every other weekend, and give her as child support – but only as child support – £1700 a month, out of which she could cover her mortgage and maintenance. This was vital for me, and I'd advise it to anyone in the same position. So long as you're giving £1100 a month in child support,

the CSA has no power to intervene, so at least you can calculate your maximum outgoings. If you get into maintenance and mortgages, or anything linked to indices and earnings, the ex can keep hitting you for more.

Anyway, we agreed to live in the same house while we sorted out the property logistics. (I'd keep out of the way, getting gigs out of town and so on.) We also agreed that she could sue for divorce on grounds of unreasonable behaviour: 'Say I was a sex maniac,' I joked, 'or a workaholic'. But within a week, I was served with the papers in my own home, alleging that I was so aggressive, Nicky was scared of me; that I was violent to the children; and that I had been withholding money. What money?

There was no need for cruelty, so I made her attach another charge, of adultery with an unnamed other. (In court, I denied the former and untruthfully confessed the latter.) But that was child's play, compared with the money question. My tactics there were quite clever. When I sold the five-bedroom house and bought her a four-bedroom place, I'd done it with agreement on both sides that I would have a 20 per cent charge on her home, once Luke was 18. That was in recognition of the fact that I'd given her the lion's share of the capital. Now I offered to drop the charge if she agreed to the child support deal.

Until then, her solicitor had been pushing for maintenance. Now he realised the game was up. He came to see me and said he'd advise Nicky to sign if I settled an outstanding

£5000 bill, which I had been challenging. I said, 'I haven't got the money, but you can have my Mercedes.' And he took it! Still, nothing could surprise me by then. Look how Nicky acquired a new man. Ten days after her house purchase was completed, she rang me and said she was with Martin. I said, 'What the fuck! Last year you denied it!' She said, 'That was then. This is now.' As if I wasn't already bitter. But at least I wasn't worried about the kid this time. I thought, 'Well, she'll be responsible for Luke, not me.'

Of course I love Luke and I want to see him, but I don't do that FNF routine. If anything, it's the reverse. Nicky rings and asks if I'll take Luke for an extra night and I say, 'Sure, I'll knock it off my quota next month.' You see, I've come to disagree with the FNF line. They believe children should have two homes. With Max, that was necessary for his safety — but it also caused him a lot of confusion. With Luke, I'm clear that his home is with his mum. Nicky keeps going on at me, saying I should have a three-bedroom place. As far as I'm concerned, Luke can share my room until Max doesn't need his any more.

Luke and I make huge amounts of stuff together out of cardboard and paste — especially carwashes and garages — but I encourage him to take it home. I don't want this flat to be his 'bubble'. Of course, Nicky tries to lay a guilt trip on me. She'd have preferred to keep me round the corner, giving her three lie-ins a week and acting as unpaid babysitter — but apart from anything else, I can't afford to

do that again. So I act nonchalant, which denies her the leverage. I've decided that if I'm happy, then Luke is happy. I'm not going to turn down work. He can fit in, and it'll make him happier. On the other hand, I'm having him to stay all next week, while his mother goes to Scotland. And I've got Max at the moment, because his mum is moving house. So I'll need to get up at 6.15 to get both kids to school.

Okay, lets get back to Max. It took a couple of years to get right. When he, Sara and Ian emigrated, Sara naturally messed me around over dates and flight times. And once I'd met Nicky, Sara claimed he didn't want anything to do with me. So I just flew over to Greece, got a taxi to their town, and phoned to announce my arrival. After ten weeks apart, I only got to spend two hours with him – in a restaurant, while Sara and Ian watched from another table – but I got him laughing, and I knew then that, whoever else had a problem, he and I didn't have one with each other.

Over the week, I built on that trust, and proved that nobody had anything to fear from my visits. Within the year, I was booking a villa for a week, and having Max to stay. It was like we'd never been parted. Because of those early years, Max and I have a very special relationship in which I, basically, play the buffoon. We even used to have this daft secret language. And I think kids who only live with their mums miss out on that. Most women are too precious about their dignity to fool around. Anyway, shortly after that, Max and Sara confided in me. Ian had been violent and

abusive to Sara, so she was going to leave him and come back to Britain. It took her until 2001, but now she has a place in Hampstead, she's had a lot of therapy, and she's learned to put Max first.

You know, after losing Max, I spent years in torment. This time round, with Luke, I've learned how to handle it. You need to do a mental trick. To stop the anxiety, you have to put it in a mental 'box', which you only open when you're with the child. That way, you can function. But actually, the worry still worms away in your subconscious. It begins to affect other departments of your brain. I discovered that in therapy, and now I have a mantra I say when I come across problems – even ones that don't appear to be about Max or Luke. I say, 'My kids are okay, my kids are okay,' over and over, and things begin to seem bearable.

The funny thing is, if I'd only had the first marriage, I think I would have been quite damaged by the experience. But going through it twice gives you a better perspective of what's right and what's wrong. Of course, Nicky is still doing her thing. Because I've been ill recently, I haven't worked so much, so I've reduced the child support to £1300 a month until I'm better. And she's gone up the wall. She's sent emails to all my friends, alleging that I'm a skinflint who's not interested in Luke. She's been bombarding me with weird messages about how I'm a woman trapped in a man's body, and how that means I resent her and seek vengeance. Frankly, it's water off a duck's back. Her

kind of behaviour can turn some 'contact parents' into extremists. But I'm happy not to have gone that way. After all, everything's muddling along.

5. STEVE

'I never abused my daughter when we had that
bath – but what if the mud sticks?'

23 November 2004

*Although Steve, 36, bears a passing resemblance to REM's singer
Michael Stipe, his rock'n'roll years in his native Reading are long
gone. With his girlfriend Kerry, he now co-manages the branch of a
quite tasteful restaurant chain in Bath. Working 100 hours a week
between them, they earn a joint salary of £55,000, and live rent-
free in a rambling, cheaply furnished company flat. He has two
children: a five-year-old daughter, Becky, by his ex-partner Angie,
33; and a four-year-old son, Alan, from a brief affair with Ruth,
24. Becky and her mother live in Angie's native Swansea, about
two hours' drive west; Ruth and Alan in Reading, about 90
minutes east.*

Steve chooses not to see Alan (for whom he is willing to pay

child support, when required next year). On the other hand, Angie has prevented him from seeing Becky since May 2003, when she alleged that he had sexually abused their daughter. Although her claim came to nothing, Angie used it as a pretext for banning contact. As a result, Steve withheld the £150 monthly payments that he used to give her under an informal arrangement, and took the case to court.

A month ago, after several hearings, Steve withdrew from proceedings – partly because he could no longer afford the solicitor's fees to fight his ex (who receives legal aid). He may take up the case again next year, as a litigant in person. Throughout the conversation, he keeps on the kitchen table a framed photograph of the cuddly little Becky aged four. Dressed in pressed denim, sipping a mug of tea, he seems surprisingly calm – an attitude he attributes to the help of his girlfriend, and to the psychotherapy he receives courtesy of his company health insurance...

***

My life would have been so different if my fiancée hadn't died from meningitis about ten years ago. Thanks to my therapist, I've dealt with that now, and I've learned how it influenced my later behaviour. But to fill you in, she was called Clare, and we'd been living together in Reading for a couple of years. We'd got a mortgage on a flat, life assurance, and then – bang – she was gone.

I was working in a big hotel kitchen at the time, and I

guess I found a shoulder to cry on. I started going out with a receptionist called Lucy, we got a joint mortgage, and I found myself drifting towards marriage again. I knew that was making me unhappy, so I broke it off in 1997. We sold up and split the proceeds. I quit my job and moved out of town, to a country cottage. I needed some head-space – I still hadn't got over Clare – and since I had plenty of money in the bank, I got by doing a bit of painting and decorating. And I probably had a bit too much fun.

I got off with Angie in a club. She was a bit of a character around town, a doper, pretty hardcore. She came from Swansea, where her mum and step-dad live, but had followed a mate down to Reading. She got by on income support, the odd cash in hand job, and other people's generosity, but she had a lot of charisma. And the mood I was in, she was perfect for me. It was stormy from the first – we broke up all the time – but very exciting. A lot of substances were consumed. We were both free spirits. To be honest, sometimes we couldn't have planned the next day, let alone a child.

We didn't bother with protected sex or the Pill. You might say that was irresponsible, but Angie had some problem with her womb, which halved her chances. Maybe that was why she was so keen to keep Becky, when she got pregnant in 1998. I definitely was. I can't say why, I just had a feeling. But I don't think either of us thought much about our own relationship. I didn't love Angie – I think

something died inside me when Clare died – but I did miss her when she wasn't around.

It sounds daft, but I felt, somehow, that we could 'use' Becky, if you like, to bring us closer together. I talked to my mum about it – she's divorced and remarried herself – and I had her support. But if I'd known Angie's mum then, I might have been more worried. She's also remarried – to a nice, pretty useless guy – but I think she hates men, really. Her first husband walked out on them when Angie was three months old, and I think she's transferred her bitterness onto me.

With a baby on the way, I had to think about our future lifestyle: the cottage would be too small for the three of us, and we'd need a decent income. In the meantime, I got a job managing a pizza place, and Angie moved in with me. It was probably the best three months we had – it was a lovely Christmas. Then she headed back to Swansea, where her parents could look after her, while I got things together in Reading.

I had an idea for a new business – I'd take the restaurant upmarket – so I came to an arrangement with my employer: he gave me a three-year lease in return for 60 grand at the end of the term. There was a flat included in the property, where Angie and I would set up home – so I started doing that up as well, renting in town in the meantime.

The plan was that we'd see each other at weekends. Either I'd go up or she'd come down. But to be honest, the

whole thing was crazy, because I was in start-up mode. For the first year or so, I was knackered but the restaurant was doing really well. I became a bit of a face around town, and I started snorting too much coke. (Only a gram or two a week, but that's enough to fuck your head up.) But what really did for me were the costs. I didn't watch them closely enough until it was too late. For example, I started building up a wine cellar, but the good ones moved too slowly, and the general public was scared off by the image. My private life didn't help either – that is, what life I had when I wasn't working.

In January 1999, our relationship had taken a new twist. As I say, we were always splitting up and getting back together again, but after her New Year's trip to Swansea, she told me she'd once slept with someone during an 'off' period. I guess she felt guilty, and now I can give her respect for that. But at the time, I just felt angry. I'm not proud of it, but I started screwing around myself. Over the next year or two, I had about ten flings. One of them – Ruth – I started seeing in the summer, not long after Becky was born, and by Christmas she was pregnant.

It was a crazy time. I'd opened the restaurant in May, four days before Becky's birth. Every time Angie came down, she'd say she was going to move in, then we'd have a row and she'd split. (The lads in the kitchen were placing bets on how long she would last!) And now I had to deal with Ruth. Well, I don't have a problem with abortion, but

I don't believe it's a woman's right to choose. It should be a joint decision, and if a woman decides to go it alone, she can't expect any help from the man. Luckily, when Ruth hit me for CSA payments, I wasn't earning anything – but we'll come to that. First of all, I had to tell Angie, who was finally going to move in the next time she came down.

It would be Christmas again, wouldn't it? I made sure I didn't spoil the holiday any more than our usual ups and downs did, but in January 2000, I broke the news. I tried to tell her that I wanted to make a go of things, that I wasn't interested in Ruth, but she wouldn't listen. I think she had post-natal depression. Anyway, she moved straight out, finding a room for herself and Becky in a friend's flat.

The only light in my life for the next ten months was Becky, who I had on Wednesday and Thursday nights, picking her up and dropping her off at the nursery. And Angie was happy with monthly payments of £150 cash, because it meant she could claim extra benefits and allege I was an absent father. But she was still a nightmare, and so was life. The business was going down the toilet – by the end of the lease, I was broke and I owed my old boss £25,000 – and Ruth was on my case. I'd told her that I'd give no financial support, but I didn't want to be a complete bastard, so I went to the birth in October.

For that, I got some friend of Angie's throwing a brick through my window – she knows some very heavy people – and I found myself in a bad place with Ruth. Once a

week, I'd go round to spend some time with her little Alan – I was only trying to do the right thing – but I just couldn't bond with him. I hadn't wanted him and I didn't love him. So I'd turn up for a Sunday afternoon, and after an hour or two, I'd be falling asleep out of boredom and fatigue. It was completely different from being with Becky, and I wish I'd never bothered, as it only encouraged Ruth's hopes. Now, as far as I'm concerned, I don't have a son. I never did. I never will. And I'm quite bitter about the stress that Ruth put me under, when I couldn't cope.

By March 2002, she had failed to get anything from me through the CSA – though that will be reviewed next spring, when I'm happy to pay – and I was ready for bankruptcy. Instead, my old boss offered me a great deal. He had a small hotel in Swindon and he had faith in me, so in June, he appointed me assistant manager there and gave me a room. He docked £150 a month off my salary to repay the debt – actually writing it off a year later, when I left – and he introduced me to my current partner. In fact, Kerry had done my job before me, and had gone off to be a manager with a big chain. She dropped by for a quick induction session, gave me a tour round town, and we clicked.

Angie had moved back to Swansea by then, renting a two-bedroom flat near her parents; and because of the Swindon job, we'd changed the contact pattern to two nights every third weekend. I'd pick Becky up at lunchtime on Friday and return her for tea on Sunday night. Also, I'd

call Becky every Saturday, at 6.30 in the evening, though Angie soon messed me about on that. Theoretically, everything was legally sorted. We both used solicitors to draw up the arrangement – so technically, it's still binding – but I hadn't realised that, emotionally, it wasn't.

I was just enjoying my 'Becky time'. When I took her back to Reading, it was brilliant. By day, we'd go to feed the donkeys and pick flowers. In the evening, we'd go round to my mum's to watch videos, and I'd cook her something. (Despite living in a hotel, it was about the only time I had a proper meal!) Then she'd spend the nights there. But when I was in Swansea, I didn't play it cool enough with Angie.

My mum always said, 'Keep your distance. Don't go into the house. Reduce contact with Angie to a minimum.' And she was right. But it's like there was unfinished business. Even when we were arguing, there was still something very intense going on, something that I didn't want to tell Kerry about. I didn't want Angie to know about Kerry, either. You'll understand why if I explain what happened when she did discover in October: the next time I was in Reading, she got one of her mates to scratch my car all down one side. Meanwhile, Kerry and I started to get abusive texts and calls from numbers we didn't recognise.

I should have learned my lesson, but there was something nice about the whole family all being together. I went up to Swansea that Christmas, sleeping on the floor of a friend of Angie's. Because of the blizzards, I had to stay an

extra couple of days, and we had a really good time. A few weeks later, I took Kerry up for a day, to meet Angie and Becky – and Becky really liked her. But it's never been the same since then. In fact, it's only got worse.

The trouble is, rejection is unforgivable in Angie's mind. Her mother brought her up to think that way. So when I went back to my life with Kerry, Angie shifted into a new gear. She started making up excuses that Becky was ill. Once, I drove up there and they had gone out. Between March, when I moved into Kerry's flat in Swindon, and May, when the alleged abuse took place, I went six weeks without seeing Becky. Since then, I've never seen her again.

So this is what happened. On that Wednesday in May, Angie rang up saying that Becks was poorly and probably wouldn't be fit to travel on Friday. 'Here we go,' I thought. 'Play the game, keep calm.' I drove up there anyway on Friday lunchtime and rang the bell. Angie let me in and offered me a coffee. While she was in the kitchen, Becky came in, and I asked how she was. 'Mummy says I'm not well,' she said. 'Don't worry, darling,' I said. 'Get your bag, and if there's any problem, we'll just turn round.'

What a journey. I don't think Angie could handle Becky spending time with Kerry and me. I reckon she wanted to keep me in Swansea overnight. Every few minutes, she was texting me. You know: 'If Becky is fretting, bring her straight back… If the traffic is bad, turn round.' In fact, Kerry was on the night shift that weekend. So when we got

back to her place, I cooked Becky some tea and ran a bath. I know, I know. Hindsight's a wonderful thing. But to be honest, I'd do it again. I've never been uptight about naked-ness, and I don't think children should be, either. When she had last stayed alone with me, aged three, we had our baths together. And to both of us, it seemed completely natural.

So I had my back to the taps, and she was at the smooth end. Angie had given me some nit shampoo, because Becky had caught them at school. I was under instructions to wash her hair and comb it thoroughly, so I did what I'd always done before. I pulled her up on top of me, so that she could hide her eyes in my chest, and I shampooed and rinsed her. I don't know if she noticed my genitals, but it wouldn't have been a big deal. When she was three, she used to laugh if they were showing. She'd say: 'Your willy's sticking out of the water.'

Once she was in her pyjamas, it was bedtime. Now we had a spare room for her, but she wanted to sleep with me. Mum says I should have forbidden it, but you know what kids are like. I'd tried with Becky before, and she'd still crept in. So I put her in our bed, where I joined her later. On Saturday, we picked up Kerry and went to a country village, where some friends have two girls around Becky's age. They've got a pool, too, and we had a lovely day, with a barbecue. When Kerry left for work, I took Becky home, and went through the same routine: supper, bath together, bed.

The next day, after a brilliant Sunday lunch at my mum's in Reading, I drove her back to Swansea. 'See you next time, then,' said Angie. She was really friendly, and I was gobsmacked. Normally I felt beaten down on the drive back. But this time, I was on an emotional high. I remember, when I got in, I said to Kerry: 'That went like a dream.' But the next morning, there was a text on my mobile: 'I suggest you get in touch in the next 24 hours.'

Here we go, I thought. Kerry told me to ignore her, but I reckoned Angie might be making a fuss because Becky had bruised herself on the Saturday. I texted back: 'If it's that important, you get in touch.' She did actually ring after that, but when Kerry answered, Angie said, 'Fuck off, Kerry', and put the phone down. So next, my mum left a message on her mobile, asking what was wrong, but got no reply. I decided that Angie could do with a couple of months to cool off.

You see, at exactly the same time, Kerry and I were embarking on a new life. We'd applied for the management of this place, and been given the job, starting in June. Then there was a hitch with the redecoration, and we were asked to do three months' relief management in the Cardiff branch. Although that was even closer to Swansea, it meant we could only get down to Reading and Swindon one night a week. Our lives were all over the place, and we could only give so much time to chasing Angie. Eventually, my mum got hold of her — and that's when nine weeks of high

anxiety started. Angie told her that something had happened between Becky and me in the bath, and that she couldn't say more, 'as it might jeopardise the case'. When I heard that, my first reaction was to contact a solicitor, and he wrote to Angie, asking for further details.

There was no reply, but a few days later, the Swansea police left a message on my Swindon phone. By the time I received and returned it, the guy had gone on holiday. So I left my mobile number, and a couple more weeks went by. Then he left his, then I got back and a new person had been assigned, then the case was moved around from authority to authority – until I ended up being interviewed in Swindon that August. The first thing they said was: 'Why haven't you brought a solicitor?' Then they read me my rights, without telling me why, and asked me to describe that weekend with Becky. About ten minutes from the end, they told me the allegation. According to Angie, Becky had told her: 'Daddy tickled my bum with his willy in the bath, and said not to tell you.'

I can imagine how it happened. Becky will have been describing her weekend, and got to bath time. Then maybe her mum said, 'And daddy got in with you? Did he touch you with his willy? Did he put it near your bum?' And I can imagine Becky saying yes, and Angie freaking out, and Becky trying to humour her by agreeing that I'd made it a secret. I can imagine it all. Angie rings her mum, and her mum whips things up. To be honest, I think everything got

out of hand. I don't believe that Angie thinks I'm an abuser. She's just gone in too deep with her mum, and she can't get out. I can't hate her – in a twisted way, it shows a kind of love for me – but I'll always hate her mother for making it worse.

When I heard the allegation, I felt angry, a bit shaky. But above all, I was stunned. I was just hoping that the police would see I was straight – and in fact, one of them said, 'Looking at this, you won't hear from us again.' But what I didn't realise was that didn't mean I was innocent, as far as they were concerned. It just meant they hadn't collected enough evidence to prosecute me. They said they would ring Angie. I asked if they had talked to Becky, and they said, 'We can't. She's too young.'

Still, for a couple of weeks, I felt a huge release. It had been a terrible strain on my mind and my relationship. Then the threatening messages started again. One from her mother went: 'I know you did it. I'll tell your employer. I'll destroy you.' I called her local police after that. I gave them the history and they were great this time. 'Do you want her arrested?' they said. I said no, of course, but I got a crime number, and they made a house call on Angie. They told her, 'If you or any of your family threatens him again, we'll arrest *you*.'

That seemed to scare some sense into them, and for three months, I thought things were going relatively well. I'd stopped sending any child support money in July, and I

wasn't going to start again until I knew we were sorted. Kerry and I moved here, to Bath, changed all our phone numbers and went ex-directory. I decided I'd let things cool down and just maintain indirect contact until the New Year. Every payday since June, I'd been sending Becky a letter and some photos and magazines, and every three weeks an extra card to keep those 'daddy weekends' special.

I stopped when my mum learned from Angie's that they were going straight in the bin. About the same time, I had a bit of a crisis. But since then, I've started a special box for Becky, which I can show her one day. FNF suggests it: you put all the presents and letters that your kids won't see in there for them. You open a bank account and keep it in there. I write a daily diary, too – not just to record all the proceedings, but so I can explain how things happened and how I felt. It's a kind of emotional insurance – and I needed some of that after this New Year.

I was in a bad way. On New Year's Eve, I was meant to be leading the staff in 'Auld Lang Syne'. Instead, I hid in the basement. I was crying too much to face them. And though my mental state got worse – in April, the BUPA doctor referred me to a therapist – there was some hope on the horizon. In early January, my mum drove over to see Becky at her grandmother's.

When she got the chance, while Angie's mum was in the loo, she told Becky: 'Your daddy loves you very much.' And Becky said: 'Mummy won't let me see him.' My mum

asked why, and Becky said she didn't know.

After that, my mum got in touch with Swansea social services, and they arranged to interview Becky. They didn't put her any leading questions, and it was clear to them that Becky wasn't scared of me. But even so, they said they couldn't be sure nothing had happened. That's always the way. You never get any sympathy. It's too sensitive an issue. There's never enough evidence to actually clear you. Everyone is so worried about covering their own arse, in case there's a mistake and an inquiry. So you're pushed in a corner and left to hang. I know I never abused my daughter when we had that bath, but what if the mud sticks?'

Anyway, after that, I decided to fight for contact through the courts. So I went back to the solicitor, who quoted me two to three grand for a result, and we had three hearings between April and August, starting with a magistrate. He immediately referred the case to a higher court a month later; and at that, we asked for interim contact pending reports. Angie refused it, so the judge ordered us to each prepare a statement, and for a report from Swansea social services.

We had six weeks to get it together, and I blocked off three weeks' holiday to prepare. But during that period, I began to give up hope. I could see that Angie would just drag things out – after all, she was on legal aid – so I decided I would write a report and respond to hers, but withdraw any requests for directions. As Kerry said, if

you take away the fight from Angie, she's got nothing left – because that's her way of keeping control. She said, 'You may get contact, you may never see Becky again. But Angie will have you where she wants you if you keep fighting, and you mustn't let her.'

So in August, I sent off my papers, expecting nothing more. But then my solicitor's agent rang from the court. Swansea social services were enough on my side to recommend that contact should continue – six weekly sessions at a centre for six hours a time – with a court review after that. I agreed, but again Angie said no. She wanted a more detailed report from social services – with all three of us interviewed separately – so the judge set a new date for October.

Part of me was looking forward to it. I reckoned that at least I'd see Becky at a contact centre. Actually, after all Angie's psycho behaviour, I thought I'd prefer initial contact in a centre. (God knows what would have happened if I'd turned up to collect Becky.) But soon after, when my mum received a confidential call from a Swansea social worker, I started to worry. I'd already got a quote from the lawyer. For a two-day hearing with barristers and expenses, I'd need £4000. Now this guy was saying that he thought, whatever the court ordered, Angie would act in bad faith. For example, her parents had already bought her a cottage further down the coast without informing anyone.

Well, I couldn't handle the stress, or the cost, of another court case for no definite result. Social services never interviewed me – and when the report arrived and I read it, I could tell that Angie was already manipulating the system. Yes, Becky had been interviewed on her own – and she said she missed me, and that seeing me would make her 'very happy'. But set against that Angie's claim that our relationship only ended in June 2003! Or her allegation that she'd done all the driving for a year. If she was going to start on the wrong foot, she'd continue that way. And what faith could I have in a system that never even asked for my version of events? I just didn't have the strength to fight last month.

I decided to withdraw from proceedings – but just for the moment. I'm allowed to pick up the case where we left it, and I haven't wasted my time. I've joined FNF. I've been to a couple of meetings, and I've learned a lot. I'd never heard of being a litigant in person before, and now I might be one! I've got all the forms ready, and it'll only cost me £90. But the fact is, while I know I'll get some kind of contact, I strongly suspect Angie won't co-operate, and then I don't know what I'll do. If you like, I'm prepared, but I don't have to commit to any particular course yet.

The thing is, I've already been through rock bottom. At the beginning of the year, I was having one good day a week. Now I only cry about once every three weeks – usually in my Becky time. And on the plus side, I reckon I

have some leverage on Angie. I reckon she daren't turn Becky against me because, if she does, I'll never pay any more child support – and she can't challenge that without admitting benefit fraud. She's already sent my mum a text, saying that I owe her a grand.

Also, maybe she and her mum know in their hearts that they can't break the bond between Becky and me. She's a very mature girl, and she knows her own mind. My mum was allowed to visit her in August, and showed her a picture of me. Apparently, Becky said very proudly, 'That's my daddy!'

Now, when I hear news like that, I know my fight isn't over yet. But another little voice tells me it'll never be over.

6. MILES

'The second time, their grandfather drove off with
my boys and never came back. He couldn't let a
black man win.'

11 December 2004

*In many ways, Miles, 40, is a black success story. A first-generation
Briton, whose parents hailed from Jamaica, he became an extremely skilled auto-engineer, restorer and stylist. And until his family
problems became overwhelming, he often lived a high life of fast
cars and fancy restaurants. The only traces now are an impressive
stereo system in his sitting room and an incongruous pair of riding
boots in the hall. The setting is an anonymous, three-bedroom
purpose-built flat on the outskirts of south Cambridge.*

*Miles has a girl and two boys from two failed relationships.
Jane, 14, lives with his first partner Natalie, 37, in his native
Leeds. Seven-year-old Dustin and three-year-old Craig live with*

his ex-wife Lucinda, 27, in Watford. But Miles has all three to stay on a regular basis — Natalie by mutual arrangement, the boys for two nights every third weekend. He believes all his children want to live with him full-time and that this 'will happen in the next couple of years'. He intends to appeal against the current contact arrangements for the boys, but is currently gathering his strength after a series of bruising court battles.

Deeply in debt, and trying to start a new business, Miles is not obliged to pay CSA contributions, but manages to find money 'for whatever the kids need' out of cash payments for private jobs. As a proud man, it's not a position he relishes. His mother belongs to the Maroons, a respected Jamaican clan, and he was brought up in a Christian household. Unimpressed by 'rude boy' or Rasta culture, he would rather leave broken hearts behind him, than broken homes.

Compact, lithe, his head shaved, Miles has soulful eyes and an air of sincerity that certain women apparently find irresistible. However, he says he is tired of 'playing the stud for white girls' fantasies'. For the last couple of years, he has been looking for a 'spiritual connection' without success. He staves off depression — for which he refused Prozac in 2001 — by a strict regime of exercise and yoga...

***

Sometimes, being black has had nothing to do with my situation. Often, it's meant everything. For example, Lucinda wanted to be a bad girl. She wanted a black man. But her

parents hated me for the same reason. And while the Leeds court was fine, I reckon the judge in Watford had no intention of letting a black father be involved in raising his kids when the posh white mother objected. Here in Cambridge, I've had trouble, too. If you pretend to be an African student, you might get help with housing. But when I asked the council for somewhere with three bedrooms, because I was a black single father, it was like: 'We know your type.'

I'll tell you a strange thing, too. I've never been out with a black girl. They're too aggressive for me. They know what black guys can be like, so they give you a lot of hassle. You know, with a black girl, you're working uphill. Sometimes I think that's why so many black guys don't see their kids any more if they leave home, or get chucked out. It's not just about poverty or history; it's about pride. There's too much in our race altogether. No one ever backs down, or says, 'Okay, I've got nothing to prove. Let it go.'

Natalie wasn't like that at all, when I first met her. She was very gentle, quite shy. She was part of a gang that I knew in Somerset. One night in 1986, there was a party down there and one of her house-mates jumped her. She was very freaked out. I found her sitting on her own doorstep and took her back to where I was staying. I offered her my bed, and said I'd take the sofa, but in fact we sat up talking all night – and all the next day, until I took her out for dinner. Our backgrounds were very different. I was part of a huge, extended family who were all extremely close.

She only had her sister, who was a single mum. She didn't talk to her mother or stepfather much, and she had a grudge against the real father who'd abandoned her. But we really had a rapport. We were in love.

I was living with my parents in Leeds at the time, and I was between jobs, just doing bits and pieces. I invited Natalie up, and my dad helped us get a flat through a client of his. (He's an electrician, and he knows a lot of landlords.) When we moved in, I went on the dole and we got the rent paid by the DSS. We just wanted to be together all the time. It was the real thing, and we wanted to taste it as much as possible. And for a year or so, we were very happy. We didn't need much money because we had each other.

By early 1988, I was tired of the life. My savings had run out, and we were just sitting there watching TV. Even the sex was like television: boring after a while. I wanted to get a job, and I wanted Natalie to find one, too. But her attitude to searching and interviews was incredibly negative – she gave off a kind of failure vibe – so I decided we needed a new start. (Plus, there was another reason for leaving. A friend of mine had secretly fallen in love with Natalie. Nothing had happened, but it had freaked her out.) Anyway, I'd kept in touch with a gang from Cambridge – who we'd met the year before, when we'd been to Spain – and one of them suggested I come down here and have a look around.

Well, I loved it. It's a lot more civilised than Leeds, and

everyone was really welcoming. I was actually given a rent-free room in this guy's big house – with all bills and food paid, plus £50 pocket money – in return for a bit or work on his Bugatti. Natalie was coming up and down by train and I wanted her to move in. But she said she didn't want any difficult situations arising with our landlord – and she wanted her own phone and kitchen and stuff – so we took a bed-sit in Cherry Hinton. And things went brilliantly.

Natalie had gained in confidence and found a job as PA to an executive at a publishing house. I was in constant demand through word of mouth, and we made rapid progress. The next thing, we had a maisonette, parties in the garden, and two cars (mine was a Jag). In 1989, thanks to a neighbour, I was headhunted for an experimental engine team, on top money – and it was like: 'Is this us?' But over the next year, things started to go downhill.

At work, there was a fair bit of resentment from my managers, because I was good and I knew I was. Also, racism reared its head. The project was an Anglo-French co-operation, and there was a lot of nervousness about upsetting the foreign partners by promoting me. So they tricked me out of my job. They told me that, for the books, they were going to pay me off with two month's salary. But I should then apply to a separate English company they were starting – to develop another design – and I'd be re-hired immediately. So what happened? I rang a week later and they said, 'Sorry, there's been a problem…' I was totally

knocked back. I hated their dirty money. I wanted to burn through it as fast as I could – but that led to problems.

Natalie was getting very sure of herself. Her boss was besotted by her, and giving her little presents (which made me very suspicious). And she was on my back because money was tight. That got better, once I rented a lock-up and started working again, but there were still a lot of rows. In 1990, we had a huge argument, because she wouldn't come with my family and me to visit relations in Jamaica – and my dad was paying! We actually split up then. I said I'd move out after my holiday – and in the meantime, could she look after my stuff? But when I got back, she told me she was pregnant.

My heart was thumping. I didn't know anyone else who had kids, and I wasn't entirely sure this one was mine. So I didn't let on to anybody until the birth, not even to my parents, and I just kept all this stuff bottled up inside me. At the same time, I felt sorry for Natalie – she seemed very sad about me leaving – so I told her I'd stay for the sake of her and our kid. I asked her if she'd come to the jeweller's, so she could be measured for a ring, but she said: 'I don't want to get married. It didn't do much for my mum or my sister.' And from then, her attitude started to change. The vibe I got was 'This baby is nothing to do with you.' I'd thought I could turn things round. But by now, she was really big and I was just biding my time, waiting to see what colour the baby would be.

One morning in May, I went to work as usual, and about midday, her boss came rushing in, saying: 'Where is she? What have you done with her? I'm calling the police!' I don't know what he thought I was like. I said, 'You can do what you want, but get the fuck off my property.' It turned out that Natalie had disappeared. I figured she must have gone to Somerset – but this was in the days before mobiles, and I didn't have numbers or addresses for her family.

It was five days until she phoned me. She said, 'I've had a little baby. She's so sweet, and she's got your feet.' (Like my dad and me, Jane has webs between her fourth and fifth toes.) She was only five pounds – born by Caesarian section – but Natalie didn't want me near her, only her family. I turned to mine then. I called my mum, and she was so supportive. Still, it was another week before I was allowed to see my daughter. And as soon as I held that podgy little angel in my arms, I was full of hope and joy. I said: 'We've really got to work on this. We should get married.' But Natalie was evasive. 'What's the point?' she said. 'I'm not going anywhere.'

I soon realised she had an agenda. Maybe she was always hoping that Jane wasn't mine. Anyway, in the registry office, we had to have a huge row before she would let me put my name on the birth certificate. (I reckon her sister was advising her. You know: 'If he's not on the certificate, you can change your name and disappear.') And for the next couple of years, there was a terrible atmosphere at home.

Work was going amazingly well again, but the only real happiness I had was that gorgeous little girl, and I was very hands-on with her. From a few months old, I was taking her up to Leeds all the time. But I need love in my life, it's like air to me. I started seeing other women, which made me feel really bad. So in 1993, when I started going out with an Ozzie girl, I separated from Natalie and moved into a smart one-bed flat a couple of miles away.

I tried to keep both sides of my life separate. I didn't want Natalie knowing about my new girlfriend, so I didn't tell her my address. But I was round to see Jane every day. It was a struggle. Natalie wouldn't look at me. Sometimes she wouldn't be in at teatime, or she wouldn't answer the door. She was on benefits and I'd try to give her money, but she wouldn't take it. I'd post it through the door, and she'd throw it after me. When my family visited, she'd accept gifts. But with me, it was like, 'I can do without you' – as if she was reliving all the crap her mum had been through.

She must have sussed that I was seeing someone, because one night, I turned up and she said, 'Get out now, or I'll call the police.' I ignored her, and picked Jane up in my arms. When Natalie went for the phone, I pulled the lead out of the wall. So she ran next door, shouting, 'When the police come, they'll have you.' She meant because I was a black man. And when they did come, there were three of them in a van. I refused to talk to them until one had gone back in. Then I told the other two that it was a domestic. I said they

could wait until I put my daughter to bed, and when I left, I told Natalie, 'You're full of crap. You're a racist.' And just to rub it in: 'I'm going to my girlfriend's.' Then I sped off in my Jag. And you could tell the police were like: 'What's a black guy doing in a car like that?'

At the end of 1993, I was on my own again, and really missing Jane. So early the next year, I put a proposition to Natalie. (We'd both got over our anger by then, and I was showing my face again.) I'd seen a three-storey house with a garage attached. So I said I'd rent it. She could have one floor, I'd have one floor, and the kitchen and sitting-room would be communal. I said I'd pay for everything. I just wanted Jane to have a better life. Maybe I was still hoping that, when she saw what a good provider I was, Natalie would come round; she'd realise that, for Jane's sake, I'd follow her to the ends of the earth. But things never got any better. Life stayed dull and flat.

The next year, I met the boys' mother. Lucinda was 17, at an A-level college and living in digs. I was 30. I'll come back to her later. For now, all you need to know is that she supported me in my later fight with Natalie. But in 1997, when I could have got custody of Jane, she said she couldn't handle bringing up my kid as well as her own. Now back to Natalie. Some time in 1995, she found out about Lucinda, and we both agreed we couldn't keep living in the same house. She said she wanted to go back to Leeds, where she had friends. She also wanted my mum's help in

bringing up Jane, and that was fine by me. It meant my mum could keep an eye on things. So it was agreed they should both live with my parents. I could visit Jane whenever I liked, and take her off for weekends.

That actually worked for about a year. Then Natalie started saying she felt trapped and wanted her own space. And one night, she did a flit. She rang my mum to say she was still in Leeds. A bit later, she sent her a photograph of Jane, in her school uniform – and that's how I tracked her down in the end. I hired a solicitor and he wrote to the school, explaining the situation and that I had parental rights. Once we had her address, we served a summons on her. And after several adjournments, there were two hearings.

At the first, I applied to have Jane every other weekend, plus half the holidays, any phone calls I wanted and access to the school. Natalie didn't even come that time, so I went round to knock her up. As luck had it, she wasn't in but the neighbours were. And what they said came as a bit of a shock. Natalie was on the game. These neighbours had made complaints to the police. They had car registrations, times of men calling, everything. You'd be surprised how many women do a bit on the side. It's easy money. But I think it's made her a very hard person.

In hindsight, I've realised what I should have done. I should have told the court about the prostitution, and had Jane put in my mum's care. (After all, she'd been looking

after them both.) Instead, because I had the power, I dropped my guard. The neighbours had given me her number. So before we went into court the next time, I called Natalie and told her I knew she was a whore. I said I didn't want any trouble, Jane would be provided for, but I didn't want any crap about the CSA. I had a new family to look after, and the neighbours knew her game, so she'd better find a proper job.

'I'll stop you seeing her,' she said. So I said, 'Well, I'll see you in court.' And when she did turn up, she looked such a tart, with her skirt round her waist. But she didn't give me any trouble about contact – never has. However bitter and twisted she is, she's never flouted the arrangements. Maybe she's scared I'll tell the guy she's with now about her old occupation. Anyway, she knows that if she crosses me, I'll just take Jane away from her and leave her with my parents.

So, on to Lucinda. One day, she saw me working on my Lotus. (I'd sold the Jag.) We got chatting, met up for a drink, and fell passionately in love. I've never known anything so intense. She wanted every bit of me. She even wanted my sweat. She'd drop by the garage, push me into the office and we'd have sex on the desk. Every day was unbelievable – but there were some clouds on the horizon. I was getting lazy, enjoying myself too much, so I scaled down to a studio flat and rented a lock-up. (And remember, this was the time that I was first facing court with Natalie, so I didn't want to have too much income, in case the CSA

got involved.) Also, there were Lucinda's parents.

Her mum and dad didn't get on. He hated her; I don't know why, and she was suspicious of him. When they came to visit Lucinda at her digs, they always came separately. He was a diplomat, with a lot of connections in the Far East, and they had a big country house near Radlett, full of pictures of them with VIPs and royalty. There was a lot of control in that family, but not much love. When we went to visit, you could tell they disapproved of the relationship (especially because, every time I went to my room, Lucinda sneaked in after me for sex). But I'd say their attitude was: 'This is a phase that she'll grow out of.'

That only drove us closer together. In fact, I often think she just had the kids out of pride, and then despised them. But anyway, in February 1997, Lucinda announced she was pregnant. She seemed as happy as me, and she had this rosy future painted for us. She wanted to get engaged straight away and married after she'd done her degree. She was going to study Chinese, then teach English to private clients in Cambridge. With her father's contacts she could make a fortune. And once I got my act together, I could too.

I had her finger measured for rings, and Lucinda was over the moon. Her parents, on the other hand, tried to turn her against me. They said if she left me, they'd buy a cottage for her and the baby. But in the summer, after she'd done her exams, I drove down to Radlett with an engagement ring, and went down on one knee. She said

yes, her parents freaked out, and we spent the night in a b and b. Later, I sold my Lotus and rented a little house in Cambridge, where we got married in July. Her parents didn't want anything to do with the wedding, so mine had to pay for a registry ceremony, and a blessing another time.

When we went on honeymoon to Italy, Lucinda began to unfold her plan. She said she wanted to study in Leeds, where she could stay with my parents. She said it was the nearest place she could do Chinese, with her exam grades, but that we'd see each other in holidays and every weekend. (After all, I was up there every fortnight.) This didn't sound too good to me. All my friends agreed – you can't build a marriage on sand – but what could I do? I wasn't earning enough for both of us, so I didn't feel I could stop her.

One of my friends said, 'I don't mean to be funny, but I'd tap her phone.' And I did. After Dustin was born, I got a voice-activated recorder and hid it in the sitting room. Every night, when Lucinda was asleep, I'd creep downstairs and listen, and I was really heartbroken by what I heard. She was quite often on the phone to her parents, saying things like 'I won't make my move 'til he's bought us a house'. Well, I decided not to go into the property market! But I didn't tell her whatI knew. I was so much in love. I just hoped I could turn things round.

Lucinda was turning into a real bling queen. I knew she'd been impressed by me when I had a tasty car and money for shopping and restaurants. So I figured that, if I

supported her more, she'd realise that we had a future, and chuck in the Leeds plan. I even took a five grand loan from my dad — on the never-never — to buy her a five-door car, so that she could drive up and down with the baby.

That side of things worked for a while, but she soon moved out of my parents' and went to live with my sister. She said my mum and dad were always watching her, and she felt uncomfortable with the way Natalie and Jane came round most days. 'You wanted it,' I said. Still, I figured my sister might talk some sense into her, so I paid Lucinda's rent. But then it turned out that loads of her friends from boarding-school were at university with her. Now I reckon that Lucinda's parents put her up to the whole Leeds thing, trying to keep her with their type of people, so that she'd go off me.

In fact, she was getting trashier all the time — partying, snorting coke. One Friday, when I was getting the baby seat out of her car, I smelt weed. I would have been furious if she'd been driving and smoking with Dustin in there. But obviously, she'd had someone else in the car. I could see tiny spliff burns on the passenger seat. There was ash on the passenger floor, too. That night, I went through Lucinda's address book, and found a number with an address but no name. It was the only one like that, so I rang it. 'Who's that?' I said. 'It's Adrian,' he said. 'Well,' I said, 'I'm Lucinda's husband, motherfucker, and I'm paying you a visit.' I drove up there and then, before dawn. And I'm not

kidding, by the time I got to his digs, he'd packed his suitcase and split!

When I confronted Lucinda, she said I was making something out of nothing – Adrian was just a good friend – but she was acting really guilty. I felt I was being driven to breaking-point, and there were more arguments and incidents. Once, when I was in Leeds, we went out with some of her friends, and they all looked kind of sorry for me. So another day, I drove up there in a hire car and spied on her. I could see her through my sister's window, just hanging out. But when I called her – as if I was in Cambridge, feeling down – she said she was too busy to listen. The final straw came when I saw her mobile bill for that month. There were loads of texts and messages to Adrian. And after she'd hung up on me that day, she'd spent half an hour talking to Adrian.

Come spring half-term in 1999, and Lucinda was down here with Dustin. I challenged her about the bill, and I wasn't interested in excuses. It was clear I wasn't her first priority, so I said: 'I'm better off without you. Get your stuff. You can leave the kid and fuck off!' She cried all night, and all the next morning. I told her: 'I'm sick of all this university shit. You've been taking the piss.'

I took her house keys and car keys – without a car, she couldn't run off with Dustin – and I handed her 50 quid. I said, 'I'm selling your car, and I expect you to be gone when I get back. It's over. Fuck off. There are plenty of nicer

women who will have me.' Well, she just hung on in there. She said she was sorry. She said she'd change her course. But I was like: 'I don't care. I'm going to find a better woman.' And everyone was on my side, saying it was time to be a man. She'd made me look like a prick.

It took about six months for me to chill. During that time, I landed a really good job in Leicester. It was a bit of a drive, but I was grossing £2000 a week. And when I got home, there would be Lucinda, saying, 'I'm glad you put your foot down. You were right to rein me in.' Now, I reckon she was being told to say that by her parents. They didn't want her in their hair. But for a while, she had me fooled. She'd turned back into the girl I first met. And life was easing up. She was really coming on to me, saying Dustin needed a little brother or sister. So I'd wake in the morning, turn over and have sex with the wife. I had money in my pocket, and life was good. Lucinda had broken down my suspicions – and in July 2000, she became pregnant again.

By the time Craig was born – and I'd delivered him! – we'd moved to a big country house near Market Harborough. At first, we were phoning each other every day. We were back in love. But within a month, I could feel the connection slipping. It was around then that I quit work, because I wasn't feeling welcome there. Also, Craig was ill. (Until he was one and a half, he needed drugs for high blood pressure, caused by Lucinda's cocaine use.) So I

started working from home again. There was less money, but I was helping with the childcare. I had been offered a plush job in Sweden – they flew us all out there to have a look – but I turned it down for Lucinda's sake. She never returned the favour.

In August 2001, she started a course in Teaching English as a Foreign Language (TEFL). She took the bus to Leicester in the afternoons and came back at night – and she started cutting up again. She was picking on me. You know: 'Why don't you get a proper job?' Meanwhile, she was suggesting that she should go out to Singapore on her own, because her father could set her up with some really rich clients. In hindsight, I think she was impressed when I was flush, but panicked when I was struggling. But by then, I was saying: 'Whatever. Do what the fuck you want.' And she did.

She started going to her parents a lot more and to London, to see her old friends. She'd be late coming back. She started provoking me at home. Once, when I was nursing Craig, she punched me in the face. I had blood dripping out of my nose and onto the baby (and Lucinda later admitted that in a CAFCASS report). I think she wanted me to slap her, so that she could claim domestic violence. She was bigging herself up so much, she couldn't back down. I figured this new self-confidence must have come from cocaine, or a new guy on the scene. In fact, it was both – and as far as I know, they're both still going on.

One Sunday, when she'd been to Watford, she called me from the train. 'Don't bother picking me up,' she said, 'I'll get the bus.' It was as if she'd rather sit on the bus calling a lover than talk to me in the car. When she got home, she went to the spare room, saying she 'needed her space', because she'd been sharing with a friend all weekend. Well, I'd had enough. As soon as she was asleep, I called her father. I told him: 'Come and get her tomorrow morning at 8.30. Her bags will be packed, so don't be late.'

The following day, I was up early and cooking breakfast. Craig was in his high chair and Dustin was playing on the floor. Lucinda came in and said, 'How sweet! You're so good to me.' 'Yeah,' I said. 'Too fucking good. Look out the window. Your dad's waiting for you.' And she didn't hesitate. She looked at the boys, said, 'Bye, mummy's going now,' and went. In the following weeks, she called once or twice, asking if she could visit the children. I said, 'You can come and stay, but I don't want you upsetting them by just dropping by for half an hour.'

The next I heard from her was through our landlord. He served an eviction order on me, so I called him to ask why. He explained that Lucinda had told him I couldn't afford the rent. In fact, I was just a month in arrears, but I decided to go along with it. It suited me if she thought I was going bust. In fact, I tried to give her that impression. I took the kids up to Leeds, liquidated my business, borrowed some garage space in Cambridge from a friend, and moved

into a bed-sit while I looked for a family home.

By Christmas 2001, I'd found a little cottage outside town, and we could move in at the beginning of January. I nipped up to Leeds for Christmas, then came back to sort out the move. On New Year's Day, I called Leeds to talk to the boys. My mum said that Lucinda's father had turned up and taken them out for the day. And you know what? He drove off and never came back. I don't think he or his wife cared about Lucinda or the kids. (They later moved to the Cotswolds and, despite their promises, left her in a council flat in Watford.) He just couldn't let a black man win.

Now I knew that if I turned up at their house, there'd be violence and the police would be called, so I went up the legal path. I'd had no problems with Natalie, so I was cool about the system. I didn't realise then that, in this country, a black man has never, ever gained residency from a white woman through the courts.

Anyway, over the next three years, there were various hearings with eight different judges. But at the first, a CAFCASS report was ordered. For me, that meant being watched for five minutes at handover time. For Lucinda, it meant they repeated the lie about her parents buying her a cottage. The outcome was an order that I should have the boys from Thursday to Sunday every week. Lucinda drove them over from Radlett in her father's car, I picked them up from McDonald's, and that worked. In September, when Dustin started at primary school, I agreed the Thursday

could be knocked off. And by Christmas 2002, it had become every fortnight and half the holidays.

In April 2003, there was a strange incident. I'd had to take Craig to hospital, because of his blood pressure, and I was sleeping there. I'd texted Lucinda, and she turned up around midnight, really out of it. She started getting really amorous, saying let's get back together, let's get it on. But I pushed her off – and after that, it was war.

The thing is, she'd hooked up with another black guy, a real low-life called Hector, who was into pimping, dealing, that kind of thing. She started turning up in his car, and he'd be giving me attitude. He was winding me up, too. Dustin played Saturday football, so this Hector would shout things like 'I'll keep your place on the team' or 'Come back soon'. And I'd say, 'What the fuck has it got to do with you?' One day, in October 2003, Craig told me that Hector had slapped Dustin on the legs until he cried. Dustin then spilled out the whole story: it was just because he hadn't heard Hector tell him to brush his teeth. I reported it to CAFCASS, the school, the police, my solicitor, Childline, but no action came of it. All I got was grief.

Three guys came up to me in a club and threatened me. Lucinda claimed she was scared I'd get violent, so handovers had to be done at Cambridge police station. And she started taking the boys to violence awareness sessions, courtesy of Watford social services. (She also kept delaying the divorce, because she wanted to allege assault and deny

adultery, but we settled on irretrievable breakdown.) I mean, it was ridiculous. When the boys came to the cottage, they'd hide their shoes, so that I couldn't take them to the handover. They'd kick and scream to stay for an extra half hour, and then Lucinda would report me. I decided they'd be better off living with me full-time. I got my family and a childminder in place, so that I could keep working, and I applied for residence.

There was a problem, though. I wouldn't reveal my address, as I didn't want Hector's heavies turning up on my doorstep. So Lucinda retaliated by withdrawing all contact. Now, after the pain she'd seen me go through for Natalie, she really shouldn't have done that. I can't just call her a bitch; it was truly wicked. In fact, there was a group of friends and relations from Leeds – ten of them – all set to drive down the M1 with machetes and put the frighteners on her and her pimp. I sharpened up my samurai sword. But in the end, I decided they weren't worth it. I even cut the sword in two, to put it beyond use. Much good it did me. At the hearing in January 2004, I was told that, if I revealed my address, I could have two phone calls a week and five hours a fortnight in a Watford contact centre to 'gradually reintroduce me to the children'. As if I needed that.

I held out until June, when I was missing the kids too much. I still wanted residence. But after CAFCASS had interviewed me and Lucinda again – saying 'it was obvious I hadn't moved on' – I was given every third weekend, with

me doing all the driving, subject to quarterly reviews.

I'm afraid that wasn't good enough. My solicitor hadn't even mentioned all the childcare I'd organised, and he was refused the right to appeal. So since then, I've been a litigant in person. I'm willing to take this to the Royal Courts of Justice, if necessary. I want a weekend every fortnight plus three half-hour phone calls a week, until I get residence. And I know I will, even if it's not through the courts. Lucinda's boyfriend will end up in prison, dead, or on the run. She'll need to disappear – and she'll put them with me because there's no one else.

The reviews have carried on, and the last two have been especially sour. The judge is clearly on Lucinda's side. For example, I lost my brother to cancer in September – and I also missed a weekend with the boys in August, because I was visiting him in hospital. Lucinda knew that. But her legal aid solicitor still claimed the missed weekend showed how I didn't really care. I explained about my brother, and the judge sneered back, 'And how is he today?' 'He passed away this morning,' I replied, and it was true. The judge knew it, but he couldn't apologise. He just said, 'Now, turning to the matter in hand…'

It hasn't got any easier since. I haven't been able to work properly, with all this going on, so money has been really tight. I had to borrow the deposit on this place – and I wouldn't have got it if a stranger hadn't lent me £400. (He was a council worker, who heard the treatment I got at the

housing office.) But the support of FNF, and of my own family, has kept me going. My parents have retired now – they live near Scarborough – but they often drive Jane down, or come to visit the boys. And of course, my children make it all worthwhile. When all four of us are together, we're an unbeatable team.

I can't wait for Jane to live here. At the moment, because she's got her own life and friends in Leeds, I only see her about once a month. But she says she wants to come, and I'm trying to make the transition easier by introducing her to some of my friends' kids. Also, I'm coaxing her to take up the violin again. I paid for a year's tuition when she was 12, but it annoyed her mum so she dropped it. Now, I've told her, if she goes back to it, I'll buy a cello and we'll learn together.

It's harder with the boys. I'd like to help Dustin with his football – or at least, go watch him – but Lucinda's boyfriend is involved and I can't trust myself to stay cool. Still, we have a great time together – we're building an electric car at the moment. The only trouble is, I so seldom see them that I try to swallow them whole. It's not just because I miss them. They miss me too. The other day, when I was on the phone to Dustin, he told me he was going to put Craig on his bike and ride over here. They're already planning their escape!

After Jane, I didn't want to end up with 'motorway kids', schlepping between two homes, but that's what's

happened. And I can't blame it on the age gap, because there are plenty of people in the same situation who make it work. A lot of it lies with the judges who — I reckon — have been nobbled by Lucinda's father, because they accept everything her lawyers say, and ignore my evidence. It's like the old boys' club are protecting a possession. They can't let a black man question a posh white girl's behaviour — and although they can see I'm not the stereotype they were expecting, they don't want to know. But in the end, I guess Lucinda is most to blame. She was led astray and now she's getting bitter. She hasn't grown up yet.

7. ALLY

'She'd taken the children and tried to kill me.
Now, with the police's help, she'd cut me off
from my parents.'

14 January 2005

Ally, 33, has an open, pleasant face, a good mind and an endearing way of shrugging off life's problems. His own are considerable. He is unemployed and his pregnant partner Liz is unable to work due to RSI. Their newly acquired council house on the unloved fringes of north-east Glasgow is almost devoid of personal possessions, because any they own might be seized by bailiffs recovering debts from their recently failed business. They themselves lost £70,000 on the venture, raising the money by re-mortgaging Liz's flat (now sold). And to top it all, Ally is seriously depressed, suffering from such debilitating symptoms as early-morning wakening and mood swings, without therapy or medication.

Because of his financial situation, Ally pays no child support to his ex, Meg, also 33. In fact, due to low earnings, he has paid almost none since 2002, when he last saw his two sons, Daniel, 13, and Toby, 12. The children now live with their mother, stepfather and two younger half-siblings, about 40 miles away — in Stirling — where Ally and Meg both grew up, and where the parents of each still live. Unfortunately, after a fracas between them in Meg's neighbourhood — to which he called the police — Ally has been warned that if he is seen anywhere near her house, he will be arrested. However, unless he takes a detour of several miles, he cannot visit his parents without passing her street.

There is little work in Ally's area, and inadequate public transport, so his battered Fiat is essential if he is to find a job. Without one, he will go bankrupt in the next few weeks. But he admits the thought of 30 per cent of his net income going in CSA payments — while being denied contact with his children — is a major disincentive. Among his few comforts are three photographs of his children, the latest showing two lanky ginger lads in kilts. His biggest consolation, he says, is that he has wasted neither time nor money on lawyers and the courts...

***

It's funny how things turn out. If my mother hadn't been so keen on splitting us up, I doubt if Meg and I would have stayed together. After attending the same school, we both left at 16, and started going out the year after. The question

was, how to sleep together? When we were 18, we thought that, if we got engaged, our parents couldn't disapprove. In fact, my mother was disgusted. She thought Meg was beneath me, and I admit she was a bit rough at the edges. Still, in those days, you could buy a flat round there for about £11,000 – so that's what we did – and actually, we never did get married.

I've had all kinds of jobs. The first proper one was as night-shift manager at a bakery. Meg worked in an electrical shop. And for a couple of years, everything was fine. We made up with our families, and Dan was born – which was great. I was between jobs, so Meg went back to work – at first, part time, then full time – and I was the main carer: bottle-feeding, nappy-changing, all of that. Occasionally, Meg would go out with the girls from the shop. But generally, we didn't drink much, and the home-body life suited us. We'd have friends round, but we were a happy little family on our own – soon, with Toby on the way. This time, I went back to work, as a supervisor at a DIY superstore.

Eventually, we were starting to get a bit claustrophobic, so we took it in turns to escape every Friday night. I'd made some friends at the store, and through them I discovered drink. I'd roll in so late that Meg was convinced I was womanising – but really, I was just on the piss. If I went to nightclubs, it was to drink, not to pull birds like my pals. You might ask why we didn't get a baby-sitter, and just go out once a fortnight. But for my part, I saw enough of Meg,

and this way I got a bit more time with the boys. I guess each of us was reluctant to leave them with anyone else, when we could be doing it ourselves.

So there was this atmosphere in the house the whole time. Meg was very, very possessive, and she couldn't get her head around what I was doing. As far as I was concerned, I'd seen how other people our age lived, and I just wanted a little bit of it once a fortnight. After being treated like I'd cheated for about a year, I would have been willing to, if a nice young lady had approached me. But actually, I was just after a good time, and the more Meg attacked me, the later I stayed out looking for one. It got to four, eight, nine in the morning before I went home.

By the time Danny was three, we were arguing about anything and everything. And though, in front of the kids, we tried to keep the lid on, they could sense it. Meg seemed to think the answer was another bairn – she'd always wanted a little girl – and I thought, with the atmosphere in the house, it was completely the wrong time. Besides, to have another child in the flat would have been unfair on the boys. I didn't trust her to keep taking the Pill, so I stopped sleeping with her. To be honest, as often as not, I was spending my nights on the couch then, anyway – because most of them ended with a row.

I'm terrible at arguments. I say what I have to say, then leave. That used to drive Meg mad. She became increasingly agitated – pushing and shoving me, going for a

135

reaction. If I'd hit her back, that would have shown I cared. But I didn't. Then, one day, I remember we were having a row at the bottom of the stairs, and Dan was crying. She picked him up and smacked him senseless on the bum, screaming at him to shut up. Now the boy needed reassurance, not punishment. So I grabbed her by the throat and pinned her to the wall. 'If you do that again,' I said, 'I'll kill you.' And at that moment, I meant it.

I realised right then that the relationship was over. She'd found a way to press my buttons, and I knew she'd do it again. So after a couple of months crashing with a friend, I rented a bed-sit round the corner, for £300 a month. I don't think the boys even noticed. At the weekends, I was there all the time they were awake. In the week, I was round at the flat by 7.30 to cook their breakfasts, and back to put them to bed at night. Usually, I'd hang around for an hour after that, because Meg and I had things about the boys to discuss. Also, now I was gone, she was behaving better. More than once, she said what a waste of money my studio was, and how I should move back in as a friend. But I didn't want so much involvement. She was only after the money, anyway.

That's what we sorted out next. The day I left, she'd been to the benefits office, and now she was getting £115 a week in single parent allowance – plus her rent and council tax – so we agreed that I'd give her £300 a month on the sly. And that worked okay until the CSA caught up with me.

It turned out that Meg had given the benefits office a false address for me, they had passed it on to the CSA, and the CSA had been sending me letters that I never received. I suppose Meg didn't want them to know about the cash. But the result was that the CSA 'fined' me £800 for not replying. I got my monthly payslip one day, and instead of £965 net, it showed £165. I spent every lunch break for a month ringing them, trying to explain there had been a mistake about the address, but all they were interested in was calculating how much I should pay Meg in future.

Well, I couldn't get her into trouble, and I couldn't pay my rent, so I had to go back home. I had no other options. Even my parents weren't speaking to me, because in their eyes I'd left my family. But this time, I went as the boys' father, not as Meg's partner. And, for a couple of months, I wasn't unhappy. Meg also found a job – the kids were with her parents by day – and at night, one of us was usually out. I started seeing one of my friends' sisters-in-law, a girl called Emily. She lived down this way, in a shared flat, so I'd drive over here two or three times a week – a good 30 miles each way – and still be back for breakfast. Meanwhile, Meg became pally with some guy. She was trying to make me jealous.

Of course, it was an untenable situation. One Saturday, early in 1996, Emily brought her nephew and niece, I brought Toby and Dan, and we went a funfair. I told the boys not to mention Emily when we got home, but Toby let

something slip – and after that, I was living on a promise. World War Three erupted. Meg said my relationship with Emily would undermine the kids' welfare. She said I couldn't take them out with Emily, because I wouldn't attend to them properly. It was obvious I couldn't lead a separate life, so I moved in with Emily.

Meg didn't make it easy. When I turned up to collect my things, she wouldn't let me in. I had to get a policeman to accompany me, and he only gave me half an hour to sling my clothes into bin-bags. He wouldn't let me take anything else, as he didn't want to get involved in arguments about whose CDs were whose. Anyway, later, Emily and I rented a bungalow near here, which I kept until 1999. I found another job – selling computers this time – and Meg had her money through the CSA.

As soon as I'd left, Meg denied me any contact, but I figured she'd soon cool off. I didn't want any more rows on the doorstep, and I was confident the kids would say they wanted to see me; then she'd have no power to stop it. And once she found a boyfriend, who slept over – he's called Bruce – that's more or less what happened. (It helped that Bruce was fighting his ex for access to his daughter.) Sometimes I'd take them back to my place. But often, when Emily was there – for reasons I'll explain – that wasn't appropriate. Instead, I'd pick them up from Meg's flat every Sunday morning and we'd walk round to my mum's for lunch. After that, Danny would be out on his BMX – he was

crazy for that bike – and Toby and I might watch a video. It was nice. I missed bath-times and bedtimes, but it was nice.

I can't really say the same for my relationship with Emily. The two years I was with her were pretty messy. I guess she was unstable, I was unhappy, and we both drank heavily. There were fights, cross-country chases, and a lot of trouble with her young son. (He lived in Norfolk with her mother, who was even crazier than she was.) Still, I managed to keep it together for my boys – I wouldn't drink on Saturdays, so that I'd be sober for Sundays – and I reached a new financial arrangement with Meg, who'd bought a new house in Stirling with Bruce, when they married in 1998. Actually, he's a nice guy, but he's under her thumb.

I'd had my own troubles with Meg – when I was between jobs again, she'd threatened to withdraw contact – but now I was doing quite well. (Using my credit cards, I'd set up a hardware store in Glasgow.) And funnily enough, she was under investigation for her benefit fraud – though no action was ever taken. Anyway, I said I'd give her £180 a month, and it was lucky I got some receipts. Otherwise, the CSA would never have believed me when she returned to being nasty.

Not that she was friendly. She and Bruce seemed to have plenty of money. They drove a better car than me, lived in a nicer place, and the boys were always dressed in designer gear. But Meg's mission in life seemed to be preventing me from having any fun. If I had a shop, then I must have

money. So when I turned up in a new pair of shoes – even though the boys were in brand-new Nikes – she'd say, 'What about buying them some?' She said that if I could afford a car, I could afford to give her more money; it didn't matter to her that it was on HP. And if I was late with her payments, due to cash flow, she got very fed up.

Still, that state of affairs didn't last long. My relationship with Emily was always stormy. She was forever running off to her sister, or her mother, and then we would have tearful reunions. Eventually, we split up for good – she went back to Norfolk – and Meg agreed I could have the boys from Friday to Sunday every other weekend. (She'd had the first of two children with Bruce by then, and probably appreciated the break.) But one night when I was on my own, Emily rang, asking me to rescue her from her mother. I'd already drunk a bottle of Scotch, and a few beers, but I still got in the car – and wrote it off before I'd even left Glasgow. When I rang Emily to explain, she said: 'Well, fuck off, then.'

Some good came of it. I gave up on Emily – and drink. I saw a GP about my depression and was prescribed Prozac. But on the other hand, I got a hefty fine and a two-year driving ban, which made contact with the boys more difficult. (It took four bus journeys to pick them up and bring them back here, so we normally just went to my mother's.) And I'm afraid I slipped into drugs: just dope, coke and E. I don't know if it was the legal drugs or the illegal ones –

but as a result, I lost interest in my shop. It was like I didn't want to make a profit out of people. So I wound up the business, and I was no better off than when I'd started.

It would have been 1999 by then, and I got a job with the Glasgow parking office, where I stayed for the next three years. In that time, I had two relationships that didn't work out – both times moving in with the girls – and without rent to pay, I had more money to spend on the boys. I was guilty about the way I'd left them, and how I was so far away if they needed me. And actually, I spent too much, on my credit cards again. The thing is, for example, Meg would spend hundreds – thousands – on their birthdays and Christmases, and I felt I had to go a couple of hundred on a bike or a football strip.

Until February 2002, everything went fine. Meg, who had another baby, got the money that we'd agreed earlier. I took the kids to my mum's every weekend, and I really worked on Toby, who'd become a little distant with me. When I got my driving licence back, we'd go on expeditions to the lochs. Well, I guess I was getting along too well for Meg. When I phoned and asked if I could swap round a weekend, so that I could go to a works do, it triggered more arguments about money.

You see, I had a problem. I'd come off the Prozac, to try and get back in touch with the 'real world'. And when I did, I realised how bad my finances were. To pay off my debts, I started working a lot of overtime – up to 30 hours a week

– but Meg thought, however hard I worked, she deserved about 25 per cent of my net income. Now, if she took that much, I would have no chance of controlling my debts. I actually wanted her to reduce my payments for six months, to £100. But 'There's no way on earth I'm agreeing to that,' she said. 'You'll never see the kids again.'

It was the same old patter, so I don't know how we got more heated, but we both ended up saying that we'd consult lawyers, to sort this out once and for all. And in a way we did. I've had no contact with the boys since. If I ring from my number, no one picks up the phone. If I ring from a withheld number, Meg answers and just slams it down.

A family friend recommended a solicitor to me, and I have to say he was dead straight. Other fathers in my situation, when I've told them about him, have been amazed by how he treated me. My first and only consultation was free, and he gave me an hour and a half of his time. He said it would cost from £5000 to £15,000, take a year and he couldn't guarantee a result. At the end of the year, I might just get an hour every month or two in a contact centre. But even if I got the usual access, there was nothing to stop Meg ignoring the order, and it might take another six months to get her back to court. And if she had a canny lawyer, he could spin it out for three years.

I couldn't believe it. It took the ground from under my feet. I didn't know the law allowed such unfairness, and I knew that Meg would fight it all the way. She actually called

me later that week, and she was gloating, saying I'd never see the boys again and that she'd put the CSA on to me. That made me suicidal, which led to my then-girlfriend finishing with me, so I ended up on a mate's couch for a few weeks. Meanwhile, the stress made me ill. I developed severe stomach pains, which would keep me off work for months at a time. (I was prescribed anti-depressants for the condition, which I didn't take.) But by the summer of 2002, I was ready for a fresh start. I rented a little cottage in the Strathblane Hills, sent Meg what cash I could, and waited for the CSA to find me.

When they did, they were totally unreasonable. They refused to discount the payments I was making on the car, even though I'd be unable to work – and therefore to pay Meg – without it. They wouldn't allow me a travel allowance to get to work, because the minimum range was 22 miles as the crow flies. (Although I was inside the limit, my journey was 29 miles by the time I'd negotiated all the twists and turns in the road.) They wouldn't accept the point that the overtime work was to pay my debts. When I contacted my MP to complain, they awarded me £1.08 travelling costs per day.

Luckily, it was also around then that I met Liz, at the office. She was looking to buy a flat in central Glasgow (where I would move, after a couple of months of my rural fantasy). She'd come out of a violent relationship, and she was very supportive about my situation. For instance, I'd

been sending weekly letters to the boys, and Meg had sent them back unopened with a note telling me to stop because 'they weren't interested'. So Liz encouraged me to make a 'memory box' – although, in the end, it just brought me down even further.

By late 2002, Liz was suffering a lot from her RSI. (She still has an ongoing compensation claim.) I'd stopped doing overtime, and couldn't make ends meet. And that's when we came up with the idea of taking a franchise. It's something we'd often talked about, and of course we wanted to make a big profit one day. I dreamed of building up a business that I could leave to boys, if I couldn't see them – or maybe take them into. But I must admit there was another aspect that attracted me: I could pay myself peanuts, and the CSA would have to settle for a fiver a week.

We picked on tool hire, because I knew something about the business, and I thought there was need of a place in north-east Glasgow. So we re-mortgaged Liz's flat to raise the start-up costs of £70,000, opened a branch and worked our arses off for18 months. Unfortunately, it turned out to be much harder than we thought – seven days a week – and the margins were so low, we got in a bit of a mess. If we'd stuck at it, we might have turned it round in another five years. But the prospects were too uncertain, and the energy required too much, so we decided to cut and run last September. We sold the flat to clear what debts we could, and now we're just keeping our heads down.

To be honest, by September I was in a complete state about the boys, the law, everything, and I was making mistakes at work. In May, I'd had an idea. The boys had joined the cub scouts, and they walked from their home to the hut every Wednesday evening. So if I waited for them at the end of the road, I could hand them a letter explaining how I still loved them. When we got there, I stood on the kerb, while Liz sat in the car. But by sheer bad luck, we'd arrived too early. A neighbour must have seen me and tipped off Meg because, the next thing I knew, she tore down in her car and leapt out to confront me.

She called me all the names under the sun, but I tried to stay calm. I said I wasn't there for an argument, just to see the kids. I said, 'Just give me one hour with them, and I'll never ask again.' But she wasn't having it. As I walked towards Liz, she jumped in her car and drove straight at me. If I hadn't flattened myself against a wall, she would have killed me. So I called the police. I had Liz as a witness, and I wanted Meg charged for attempted murder. In the end, they took each of us in separately, put us in different rooms and charged us both with breach of the peace. However, they said they wouldn't pursue their charges if I dropped mine against Meg. When I agreed, they let her go. But as I was leaving, one of the officers said, 'If we see you near here again, you'll be arrested.'

Again, I couldn't believe it. Meg had taken the children and tried to kill me. Now, with the police's help, she'd

effectively cut me off from my parents. I couldn't even go to the school's parent-teacher meetings, which I'd had to battle for with the boys' head teacher. I wrote to the Chief Constable to complain, but I never received a reply. And for a while, I just wasn't strong enough to take things further. It wasn't until I saw Bob Geldof's television documentary in October that I started getting fired up again. I wrote to the great and the good. I contacted Fathers 4 Justice, and we discussed several Scottish enterprises (which may yet see the light of day). I told my story on a radio phone-in show. And it was just my luck that Meg and the boys heard it all in the car.

The next week, I got a letter, forwarded from my mum's. It was in Dan's handwriting and said he wanted nothing more to do with me. I can't tell how much help he had from Meg, but one line really stood out: 'You've disappointed us too many times.' I just can't think how. Was it when I was with Emily? Was it when I tried to swap weekends? My mother is allowed to visit them very occasionally, and I'd like her to find out. But we both know that if she even mentioned me, Meg would stop her coming.

So I'm left in limbo. I hang on to the thought that Dan didn't mention Toby in his letter, but I can't take that anywhere. I just don't know how either of them feels. Are they happy? Do they ever want to see me? I don't know. Liz says I should just hang on a few years, and

they'll seek me out. But that seems like an eternity. And I can't see Meg allowing it. She'd chuck them out of home if they tried, and I don't think they'd be strong enough to stand up to her. Besides, if she's had such an effect on Dan in two years, imagine what she can do in the next three or four.

So maybe I should move away, or emigrate? But then, what if the boys needed me? People say that being denied contact with their children is like bereavement – but it's worse. You can't bring the dead back. But my kids are here. If Meg wasn't stopping me, I could be involved in their lives. I try to focus on the good memories, but my brain doesn't seem to register happy thoughts, only the pain I'm feeling. If I'd known this would be the result of leaving Meg, I would have stayed. I'd have been miserable, but at least I'd have seen my boys grow up.

In some ways, I can understand what Meg's done. She probably justifies her behaviour by saying, 'Well, I asked him to come back.' And meanwhile, the boys have got a new brother and sister. Toby calls Bruce 'Dad', as well as me. So having me on the sidelines interferes with her happy little family. I suppose I should just look forward to having my own with Liz, but it's like there's a clock ticking. Always, at the back of mind, there's the thought that I was wrong before – and if it happened this time, I don't think I could stand the pain. There have been times when I thought I could never trust a woman again,

but I didn't want to feel like that. That's one reason I'm getting married. Another is that, with the certificate, I'll have more rights over the next child.*

---

* At the time of writing, Scottish law only gives parental rights to married couples. It is in the process of being changed to conform with the English system, whereby rights are given to the father named on a child's birth certificate.

8. JONATHAN

'I've offered her £1 million so I can see Lily –
who she conceived by deception – but my ex
even ignores the courts.'

21 January 2005

Jonathan, 37, is a modest man. So one suspects that when he puts his worth at £7–8 million, he is being conservative. Not that he lives humbly. As well as a Primrose Hill flat, he owns a 150-acre 'play' farm in Buckinghamshire (complete with ancient farmhouse, horses in the stables, a tennis court, a swimming-pool and a speedboat on the lake). In his garage are a Saab, an Aston, a scrambler bike and a Harley. But there's no side about him.

In 1997, Jonathan and his ex-partner Sarah-Jane, 35, were living in Milton Keynes. The next year, within weeks of separating, she had their daughter Lily and later moved to Northampton. Jonathan bought this place to stay near them. But when Sarah-Jane

— now married — had another baby, she moved 100 miles south. Jonathan hasn't had the heart to touch Lily's room since, so it remains as she last saw it, down to the pack of Huggies behind the door. And in fact — as the blue pool table in the bare drawing-room witnesses — he hasn't really cared for the house either.

It took this farmer's son about a decade to amass his fortune. Built on property and childcare, it really began to grow after the first two years. But for the last four, Jonathan claims, it has afforded him little happiness. Until then, he had Lily for a third of her time — but he hasn't seen her at all since; and distance is little obstacle to a man with a helicopter parked in one of his barns.

After 32 court hearings, £50,000 spent on legal fees and a year as a litigant in person, Jonathan joined Fathers 4 Justice early in 2002. (Although not a typical member, neither, surprisingly, is he its richest.) Because of his activities with the group, he has gained a criminal record, which he fears will affect his entry rights to the USA and Australia, where he also has business interests.

Despite his youthful looks and gentle manner, there is a glint of steel in Jonathan's eye. Scornful of the government's recent suggestions of tagging and community punishments for recalcitrant mothers, he fully intends to change society within two years. Meanwhile, he has arranged his finances so efficiently that — despite an income of £200,000 a year — he only needs to give Sarah-Jane about £500 a month. She in turn is pursuing him through the CSA for four times as much...

You have to understand, I don't like being an activist. It may be that some guys in F4J use the whole thing as an ego boost. But I'm stopping in two years. And by then we'll have changed the law. We've already planted our agenda into the public's consciousness by our stunts. Now we're going to convince them to vote for it. But we're not going to do it through debate. Voters don't really care about policies – what matters to them is the economy – so we're going to hit them in their pockets.

Thanks to the F4J actions in Parliament and on Buckingham Palace, the security improvements will cost about £100 million. That's more than £3 tax on every working man and woman in the country. Once we've stopped the M25 a few times, the bill will have risen to £50 per person. By then, the government will be getting worried about it, and they'll appease us. They'll change the law, and the public will support them. There's no question of that. We don't contemplate defeat.

As an individual, I don't think I ever have, and I put that down to the death of my father when I was 16. He started out with two pigs and ended up farming 3000 acres – and he was a great parent, really hands-on. After that, I had something to prove. Though I was very good at sports, I was severely dyslexic. After eight private schools, the only thing I'd passed was a gallstone. But I was determined – above all

– to make money, so that I could experience the highs and lows of the world. I've gone sky-diving in Africa, and then slept in a locals' reed hut. That's what I like to do.

When I was younger, I was driven by aggression – I didn't want to be seen as a blithering idiot – and I suppose it was that energy that attracted Sarah-Jane to me in 1990. I was working in the lettings department of an estate agency in Hampstead. She was a student teacher, a petite blonde looking for a flat to rent with a friend, and I showed them round one. We started going out, and when her friend moved on, I moved in. I never envisaged it as a long-term thing, and when I went travelling the next year, we split up.

The female of the species can be very cunning. Four months later, she called me in Bali, and announced she had cancer of the womb. She was going to have treatment, she said, but could she join me for a while before her lapioscopy? (Little did I know that was part of her fertility treatment – for which I would later pay without realising.) Now if you want to kill me, you do it with kindness. Aggression? Bring it on! But our parting had been amicable, a bit sad, and what kind of bastard would say no if he were in my position?

In fact, it didn't work out. After her visit, she went back to Britain, and I kept travelling. But later, when I was on another continent, she came out again, and we picked things up. And when I got back, at the age of 24, we took a flat together in London. It was an easy option for me, I

suppose. With her continuing 'cancer treatment', I knew we wouldn't be starting a family; and I was too busy on other projects to think about anyone else. Between spells travelling and stints at the old estate agency, I was setting up on my own.

Once I'd collected about £100,000 in clients' deposits, I used that rolling fund as my own deposit on the mortgage of a derelict building and park in Milton Keynes, which I developed as office space and a 'super crèche'. (I later discovered this first speculation was an illegal use of my clients' money!) For a time, we also lived in the building; and when Sarah-Jane had free time from her job as a classroom assistant, she would sometimes help with my various businesses. In some ways, it was because of her job that I thought of going into childcare. So when I did it in 1995, I put her in charge. I was happy to make her happy – and so long as she kept an eye on the books, the business couldn't fail to make money. Under some subtle pressure from her, we also became engaged – though no date was set for a wedding.

It was just as well. Within six months, our relationship was on the slide, and a year after that, we began to split up. That's when it became clear that the childcare business was in chaos. There had been a worrying turnover of staff. Now her two key people were threatening to leave. They came to me and said: either she goes or we do. I confronted Sarah-Jane, and she admitted she'd screwed up the business. And

when I looked at the books, I was horrified. She owed about £80,000 to the Revenue, because she hadn't been paying the staff's national insurance! After that, I took over the accounts. I tore up her company credit cards, I signed all the cheques, I dealt with all the mail – and every week, I had a new surprise, a new problem that she hadn't told me about.

We kept out of each other's way for about four months after that. I went travelling for a month; then I paid for her to visit some friends abroad. One day, when she'd just come back, a friend of mine called Bill took me aside and told me that, two years before, she'd borrowed £5000 in cash off him. (She'd claimed she was doing it for me, that I was in financial trouble and too proud to ask.) He also told me she'd done the same to two more of our mates – and it says something for all of them that they didn't mention it to me.

Once I'd confirmed it with the other guys, I went home and said to Sarah-Jane that I would offer her an amnesty until midday. Anything she wanted to tell me before then would be forgotten. Anything discovered after that would be an issue. I didn't say that I knew about the loans. I guess I was testing her, but I think it was totally justified.

Come midday, and she said there was nothing more to add. Except Bill's loan, I prompted. Except that, she admitted. And the other two? And the other two. I felt a kind of hatred for her, for deceiving me when I'd been trying to help. Now I knew I was dealing with a pathological liar. But

154

I still wasn't ready for what she told me next – she was four months pregnant – and when I asked about the cancer treatment, she said she was cured. 'Oh shit!' doesn't quite cover how I felt. I rang a friend for advice, and he said, 'At least I can see a bright side.' What's that? 'It isn't me.'

Well, I tried for a few weeks, but the relationship was so shattered that it couldn't be fixed. I gave her a Mercedes and £25,000; she went back to her mother in Portsmouth – and within a month, she was engaged to a social worker from Northampton. I'm sure she must have been seeing him before we finally separated – but as a DNA test later proved, it was my baby, not his. Actually, he sounded like quite a nice guy when I once talked to him on the phone, but he said he didn't want to be involved in our dispute. I don't know if they're still together.

Anyway, Lily was born in the spring of 1998, and Sarah-Jane made me wait five days to see her. I tried to bury any acrimony that I felt – in fact, I was grateful not to be upset about Sarah-Jane's new guy – but over the weeks, a couple of things pissed me off. For example, I only found out from a mutual friend called Tony that Lily had been christened. (I dropped him after that – he should have told me before.) Still, Sarah-Jane and I semi got on for about eight months. She moved to Northampton and, as soon as Lily was big enough, I had her every weekend, plus an extra Monday a fortnight. We'd meet halfway in our cars to do the handovers. I gave Sarah-Jane £150 a week in child support,

and everything ticked along quite nicely. But over the next 18 months, she became insanely jealous of my success, as if she deserved a piece of it.

I think Sarah-Jane was angry that I'd upset her original plan, which was to back me as a winner – to marry me and have my children. Now I was going great guns without her. I sold my agency, and a development firm that I'd started, to concentrate on the childcare business – and it did phenomenally well. But from then on, there was trouble. Any disagreement on the phone, and Sarah-Jane would deny me contact and slam the receiver down.

One weekend, I brought Lily here, and we had a picnic in a field, where she got a bramble scratch on her side. So Sarah-Jane alleged child abuse, and contact was withdrawn for about six months. When the case came to court, the judge said it was a ridiculous allegation. When the guy from CAFCASS interviewed me, he agreed. On the other hand, when I told him, 'If I'm a child abuser, you should shut down my business, and then I can sue you for millions,' he replied: 'That's not relevant.'

I got a pending penal order against Sarah-Jane that time. But for the next few weeks, I was only allowed to see Lily in a contact centre, near her new home in Surrey. It was two and a half hours drive away. But when I flew there, Sarah-Jane threatened to ask for a change of location. Anyway, you've probably heard how ghastly those centres are. You've got fathers with tattoos on their eyelids standing

round the walls. A lot of them probably shouldn't be allowed to see their children under any other circumstances – I mean, they're scary. But once, when a hard case came over to talk to me, I was so focussed, I said: 'Sorry mate, but fuck off. I've only got an hour with my daughter, and that's what I want to concentrate on.'

It was very difficult. I wanted to give Lily unconditional love, but I knew I had to be a good parent, too. Now if you've got all day, you can discipline a child for not sharing a toy, say. You can watch them go off in a sulk, and you know it'll all be forgotten later. But when you've only got an hour, and there are other kids coming up to play with you, and you see your daughter from behind at the other end of the room, and you're wordlessly willing her to come back to you... It's very hard.

The only thing that's worse is to be denied all contact – so Sarah-Jane did that again. So I had to go to court for my rights again. While there, I got another meaningless penal order, and the judge told us to go to mediation. As if there was any point. I wanted the old arrangement enforced. Sarah-Jane was offering me one day a year. And – talk about a level playing-field – the mediator's proposal to me was: 'How about twice a year?' Sarah-Jane and I argued so much that, at one point, the guy asked us separately what the date and time was. When we answered, he said, 'Well, at least there's one thing you agree on.'

Actually, it was at one of those sessions that I discovered

about the cancer lie. I said something like 'the baby wasn't planned' and the guy said, 'Then why was Sarah-Jane having fertility treatment?' You could have picked my chin off the floor. Soon after that, Sarah-Jane tried another tack. In mid-2000, she began saying that Lily no longer wanted to see me; that she was having night terrors about sleeping in my house. Now this was clearly nonsense. Previously, when I'd had Lily for two weekends in a row – to fit around Sarah-Jane's diary – she'd begged not to go back to her mum. I decided I'd had enough. Instead of protecting my rights in court, I'd go on the attack.

From the first, there had been some minor matters on which we couldn't agree – and I'd referred them to the courts as amicably as I could. For example, I was unable to stop the name 'Lily', which I didn't have any connection with. But I did make sure she had my surname as well as Sarah-Jane's, so she's double-barrelled now. Also, I had to apply for parental rights, because Sarah-Jane had put 'father unknown' on the birth certificate. (Still, the DNA test sorted that out.) Now I decided to sue for residency. My aim was to use the courts to either jail Sarah-Jane or bring her to a deal.

I have no trouble remembering the date of the final hearing. It was 9/11. When I came out of the court, everyone was saying, 'Have you heard the news?" And I was thinking, 'I've got all the news I need.' It was a farce. The judge actually asked me what he should do to Sarah-Jane.

Now twice before, I hadn't asked for the enforcement of penal orders, even though that was my right. This time, I said: 'Jail her.' Otherwise, what's the point of penal orders? But he started banging on about how it would be cruel and unreasonable to separate a child from its mother.

As far as he was concerned, in the face of 'the mother's implacable hostility' to contact, he was ordering a two-year 'cooling off period' with no leave to appeal. Two years, in which Sarah-Jane was supposed to 'promote contact' – and I was limited to Christmas and birthday gifts and letters. Since then, I haven't tried to get contact through the courts – there's no point – but I haven't given up.

Last month, I had a rocking-horse delivered to Basingstoke on 20 December. Five times, Sarah-Jane refused to accept delivery. I didn't wear her down until 7 January, and by then the delivery charges had cost me more than the present. But she'd better get used to it. I'm never going to lose touch with my daughter. When Lily is about 12 and she can handle it, I'll make sure she learns what happened. And if Sarah-Jane tries to disappear, I'll put a private investigator onto her. She will feel my wrath. She'll get ten times the pain she caused me. And Lily and I will pick up our relationship, even if it takes until she's 21. She's a tough little girl. She knows her own mind. Eventually she'll demand to see me and Sarah-Jane won't be able to stop her.

You see, I've tried the conventional routes, and they got me nowhere. In fact, I wasted my time on them – and for

that I place most of the blame on the lawyers and judges. One barrister actually said to me, 'If you're looking for justice, you've come to the wrong place,' and I respected him for that. My normal experience was of some hung-over prat who hadn't looked at his brief until he got into the courtroom. The last one, before I became a litigant in person, kept calling me by Sarah-Jane's surname. Four times he did it. I wanted to hit him for his stupid arrogance.

As for the judges, they're spineless. They say their hands are tied by the law. They claim there's no special treatment. But when David Blunkett wanted the confidentiality rules overturned, they laid it on for him. Still, at least it proves that British justice can't be bought. I know a guy in the same fix as me, the head of a major UK computer company. He's spent a million on lawyers, and got no further than me.

As far as I'm concerned, the legal profession is the scum of the earth. I have several properties that I rent out, but I won't let barristers or judges near them. One sad joke to arise from our hearings was that Sarah-Jane hired a top firm of London divorce lawyers – then never paid them. (Of course, they won't take her family home with the children in it, and she has no other assets worth speaking of.) Meanwhile, a sad consequence of everything was that I had to sell the childcare business a couple of years ago. Thinking about the children made me dwell on Lily too much. I'd say to myself, 'She'll be having her lunch

now' – or whatever – and it was causing me too much pain.

I hoped to get some support from Families Need Fathers – but if you ask me, they're toothless. The only advice you ever get is 'write a letter' – to the ex, or CAFCASS, or the solicitors. As if letters make any difference. Sarah-Jane was so proud, she wouldn't back down under the threat of jail. She was willing to call the judge's bluff, rather than swallow her pride. It actually makes her happy to see me eaten up. There's a type of woman like that, and the only way to make them behave reasonably is to jail them – if necessary, one week a month, over and over.

It's funny, but for 18 months, I was depressed; and I still haven't recovered my drive for money. Yet I'm so determined to see F4J achieve its aims that I have to be careful I don't become consumed by it. I've given them a few thousand, and run marathons to raise as much again. (I don't think, as an activist, I should give more than four figures of my own. It might make the others grumble about their subscriptions, and it would give me a power over the group that I don't want to have.) My next plan is to raise some serious money from the business community. I'm involved in a digital venture that will have two of the world's richest men on its board. Now, if I can get alongside one of them, and he's been though the mill like me – or one of his sons has, or a relative – who's to say he won't donate two or three million?

You see, rich people are no different from anyone else

when it comes to their kids. None of the stuff that I've acquired means a thing to me, compared to Lily – and if I had my time again, I've realised that I'd play a different game. I would advise anyone starting on the road I've been down to roll over, never argue, eat shit. If the ex asks for £50, give her £150. If you swear, say sorry. But whatever you do, keep the mother happy.

It seems that option is no longer available to me, though. Last year, I contacted Tony – the guy who'd let me down about the christening – and asked him to put a proposition to Sarah-Jane. (I wouldn't commit anything to writing, in case she used it against me for her ongoing CSA demands.) My starting offer was £1 million to reinstate five days a fortnight. But she hates me so much she won't even consider it.

I have to stress, as far as I know Sarah-Jane is a good mother. She just has a pathological glitch, and that's her tragedy. It means her hatred for me makes her forget what is in the best interests of our daughter. For my part, I don't think I'll ever get through the hatred I feel for her. In fact, it took me a long time to have a decent relationship with anyone after we split. I acted like a bastard to girlfriends. But I was angry with women, society, everything. Now I've got a really good, decent girl. Still, all the time I find I'm checking her out, seeing if there's any downside to her. When you've offered your ex a million to see your baby – who she conceived by deception – and she even ignores a

court instruction to promote contact, it tends to make you see women as manipulators.

They're vengeful, too. Even though I have parental rights, I can't exercise them without taking legal action against third parties – and Sarah-Jane would see that as adding fuel to the flames. So I didn't sue the vicar, when he wouldn't tell me who Lily's godparents were; and I didn't sue the school (when I knew where it was) because it wouldn't send me reports or invitations to parent-teacher meetings.

Luckily, I've become reasonably good at detaching myself from emotional pain, as I did when my father died. But every now and then, reality comes along and bites me on the bum. Sometimes, it really upsets me that Lily could be ill, or a victim of bullying or something, and I wouldn't realise. And you know what really tears me apart? After all this time, she'll have grown up a lot. So if I saw her again, I probably wouldn't even recognise her.

9. RORY

'The emotional abuse of abduction abroad will
leave lifelong wounds on our children.'

29 January 2005

*From his home-haircut to his square specs, to the woolly socks that
he wears indoors, Salisbury-based Rory, 41, looks just like the
£40,000-a-year computer programmer that he really is. Living in
a three-bedroom former council house with his Madagascan wife
Manju, 38, and their seven year-old daughter Usha, he gives
no hint of his former interest in the New Age and all things
quasi-mystical.*

*Once a mainstay of the 'mind, body and spirit' circuit, he avoids
that world now. He has learned the hard way that there are too
many misguided people in it — his ex-partner Trix, 42, for example. The mother of his first two children — Sunil, 15, and Anoushka,
11 — Trix has never worked, but has occasionally earned some*

money by renting out properties provided by her parents. For the last two and a half years, she has effectively denied Rory access to their children by taking them to various foreign locations. She has now settled in southern Italy with Sunil, Anoushka and Satia, her four-year-old girl by a Tamil boyfriend who has since disappeared. Her mother also makes lengthy visits.

Rory has been trying to re-establish contact through the courts. After an action in Italy under the Hague Convention, proceedings were transferred to Britain last year. But by then, the children – with whom Rory used to be on good terms – had turned against him. He is convinced such an abrupt change signifies that they are under mental duress, and that restoring contact would limit the psychological damage.

Both Rory and Trix come from comfortable backgrounds – her father is a surgeon, his owns a telecoms business – but during their relationship, neither led settled lives, even during their better times. Rory spent many years teaching English as a foreign language (TEFL), abroad and on residential courses; Trix has been a 'traveller' since she was 18.

Although Rory has now discovered domesticity, he has yet to find peace. On various occasions, he has suffered from panic attacks and insomnia. And though the tranquilliser Temazepam brought temporary relief, his doctor preferred to prescribe a non-addictive anti-depressant. Because Prozac made him nauseous, he now takes a fairly high daily dose of Efexor. This gives him a placid demeanour, but the sleepless nights continue…

***

Let me start with the worst three days of my life, and then I'll describe how I got there. It was last September. After two years of not seeing my children, I'd flown to Brindisi airport with Guy, a CAFCASS officer, who was going to interview them, and observe me interacting with them. My children were living in a town about 30 miles away, and I'd booked a room for Guy there. He rented a car and drove. I couldn't afford a car myself – and we'd agreed that I shouldn't stay in the same place as Trix and the kids, in case I bumped into them – so I took the train to another village. In my rucksack, I had a change of clothes and some presents for the kids – Satia as well – including an enormous box of chocolates.

The next morning, before he went to see the children, Guy rang to suggest we all meet in a café at two that afternoon. I said I didn't think the café was a suitable ambience for such an important event. So we agreed on a little park opposite it. I took a taxi over to the cafe with my gifts and some stuff I wanted to show Guy, and met him there at half past one. First, he told me that, having seen the kids earlier, he wasn't very hopeful. They still said they hated me and didn't remember my mother. So he was surprised when I showed him happy pictures of them with my extended family and me, throughout their lives.

Next, he said that Sunil had told him he wanted to 'lay

166

down the law' with me. (I was looking forward to that talk, even though I knew Sunil would be angry.) I reminded Guy that I wanted him to observe me with the children separately, as well as together. My reason was that I thought Anoushka was being influenced by her brother and would act differently on her own. The way I saw it was this: Sunil had a very hostile attitude to me, but that was his way of communicating his troubles; Anoushka was just copying to placate him and her mum, but underneath she still felt very affectionately towards me.

At that moment, Trix drove up in a little Fiat; she didn't have baby Satia with her, so she must have left her with someone. Guy went over and had a quick word. Then Trix drove round to the other side of the park – I heard her stop – while the kids walked in. Guy beckoned me over, and we followed them. In the middle, there was a wooded area, and a few yards before it, Guy called out to them. They stopped, but they didn't turn round. I said, 'Hi Sunny, hi Nush.' But they didn't reply. I moved round to one side, to try and catch their eyes, but they wheeled round, to keep their backs to me. Sunil was shouting, 'We don't want to see you! We hate you!'

I knew it wouldn't be easy, but I'd never expected this. Still, I thought: 'It's okay, they're my kids. When they see me, everything will be all right.' Guy looked shocked; he'd already been very concerned by the sarcasm of Sunil's recent emails, which I'd shown him. Now he asked them to

turn round, but they wouldn't, so I talked to their backs. I had to take that opportunity. I told them I loved them, and wasn't going to steal them away from their mum. I said that the courts were only involved to help us all, not to hurt Trix, and Guy repeated it. Then he said, 'Weren't you going to tell your dad some things?' Sunil replied, 'I don't want to now.' So Guy asked me to sit down on a bench while he had another word with them. He took my presents for them, and they walked off together.

That's when I started weeping. I could see Trix hanging around by one of the gates, and I thought of going over to reason with her, but I was scared of the consequences. Besides, Guy had asked me to sit there. He came back after a few minutes without the kids – they must have been hiding in the trees – and said, 'I'd like to call this to a halt. I don't think it will benefit them to continue.' I said I'd still like to try and speak to them separately, but he wasn't happy. I asked him to consult with Trix, and when he came back, there were tears rolling down his cheeks, too. 'She's not prepared to allow it,' he said.

Guy went off to find the kids, and I just sat there. I caught a glimpse of their backs as they went towards Trix, and that was that. It was some time before he returned, and when he did, I noticed that he had my presents in his hands. That was what had kept him – the kids had thrown them around the park, and he'd been picking them up. He hadn't found the chocolates, so we went to search for

them together, and he told me how unhappy he was with Sunil's behaviour.

When we got back to the bench, we sat talking for an hour, while he made notes. In his view, the kids were too far-gone. He wouldn't be recommending a British court order, and he hoped time would heal the wounds. I took the opposite view: the longer this damage to their minds continued, the more screwed up they would become. I just couldn't believe how Anoushka had turned from a very affectionate, fun-loving girl into this little ball of hate.

Guy flew back that night. I'd booked a cheap deal, giving me an extra day in case things went well, so now I couldn't change my ticket. I was in a daze. I just wanted to be home, and I didn't know how I was going to get through it. But I portioned the time out in my mind – 'I'll eat, I'll sleep, I'll wash', and so on – and somehow made my way back.

Last November, we had the final hearing, in Brighton, and it was like a bad dream. The judge confirmed an order allowing the permanent removal of the children from the UK, so I'll never see them again. I asked him about counselling for the children, and he said there were no resources available in England or Italy. I asked if we could stop Trix from 'home schooling' – which meant no schooling – and he said he was 'powerless to intervene'. My only consolation was that he agreed there should be a joint statement, at the beginning of the order, saying that I had never applied

for the children to live with me. That was what Trix had been saying, to alienate them.

One day, I hope to show them that. Then they'll know. But in the meantime, all I've got is memories: how Sunil and I played 'Dungeons and Dragons', and how I taught him to programme games into his computer; how he and I went swimming, or Anoushka and I went cycling and roller-skating. And she used to love running through the sprinkler in the garden at home...

Anyway, how did my life get to this? Well, it started in 1985, at the University of East Anglia, when I was in the middle of a philosophy degree. Trix was crashing on the floor of her sister, who was a friend of mine, and she'd just got back from her first trip to the East. I was very attracted to her – she's an 'earth mother' type – and we became very close. When she became pregnant in 1989, we just 'went with the flow': neither of us agrees with abortion.

Because of our lifestyles, we were often apart for months, even after Sunil was born. During other periods, we lived together as a sort of family. We did have sex from time to time, but she wanted an 'open' relationship – at least, for herself – and I suppose I was under her spell. When I did have the odd affair, like with Manju in 1992, she found ways to make life difficult, such as accusing me of putting my own life before Sunil's. That's why I went back East with Trix that year. She asked me to come and

help look after him. But she warned me she was going, whether I came or not.

I got her pregnant the first night in Bangkok. It was the only time we'd slept together in years – I guess we were on a traveller's high – and also the last. I bitterly regretted it the next morning, and even more so three months later, when she turned out to be expecting. She was pretty bitter, too. We returned in 1993 and set up a platonic family home near Stow-in-the-Wold, where my parents live. Anoushka was born in September, and things were stable for about a year and a half. But by July 1995, she had hitched up with a rich Italian guy called Giovanni. She wanted to go travelling with him until the autumn and leave Sunil with me. (She was already saying she found him hard to handle.) But I said that wouldn't be good for him, so she took both kids with her.

For the next two months, I was out of my mind with worry. I had no idea where they were until October. Then she dropped in briefly, before heading for Brighton, where Giovanni lived. He had a spare flat, which he would lend her. So at the end of the year, Sunil started at school there, and Anoushka at nursery. I had a very happy Christmas with them – and an even happier New Year, because I met up with Manju again.

The rest of 1996 saw a lot of changes. Trix couldn't handle being an authority figure. She couldn't cope with getting a child to school, fed and clothed, or getting him to

bed on time. So she took Sunil out of school, pretending she was educating him at home. But that didn't help, because she was caring for Anoushka. When Sunil played up, she became very aggressive with him. I think she must have hit him. In the end, she rang me up and said, 'I'm doing him harm. You've got to take him.'

I agreed, so Sunil came to live with Manju and me in Bournemouth, where we were renting a house. He did well at school and began to build a social life, but he was very angry. He thought that Trix preferred Anoushka to him, and I could see why. Mostly, the only times he saw his mother was when I took him, on my trips to see Anoushka. Trix only came to visit him twice in 12 months. And the second time, she announced that she, Anoushka and Satia's future father intended to go travelling again – without him. On my insistence, before she took off, she signed a form giving me parental responsibility over Sunil (which turned out to be important later).

They were meant to go for four weeks. Instead, they took five months, only coming back for Satia's birth. Meanwhile, we had Usha – who both my kids loved – and Trix was bought a little house in Brighton by her mother. Once or twice, she offered to take Sunil for a jaunt, but I couldn't allow it during term-time. He did spend three weeks with her during the summer holidays of 1997, but I don't think it was good for him. Trix started talking about taking him and his sister on another big trip. She

kept raising his expectations in unrealistic ways, then letting him down.

A difficult year passed, and disaster struck the next summer holidays, when Sunil was back with Trix. She rang out of the blue to say that she and Sunil both wanted him to live with her in Brighton, starting in September. My main reaction was anxiety. So much harm could be done to Sunil if she let him down again. All the progress he had made would be jeopardised, too. I proposed that we proceed cautiously, maybe talk it through between then and Christmas, but Trix seemed impatient. The next thing I knew, Sunil was on the phone, saying: 'I'm cross with you for trying to stop me living with mummy.'

By lying to him, she'd put me in an impossible position. So very, very reluctantly, I consented. I made all sorts of verbal conditions about the encouragement and maintaining of contact with Manju, Usha and me; and about both kids continuing in state education. I didn't want to leave any concerns unaddressed, so I went into some detail – teeth to be cleaned twice a day, high-factor sun screen to be used, and so on – and Trix agreed to them all. Manju and I even thought of moving near Brighton, to make weekend visits easier. But it seemed crazy to settle anywhere on the assumption that Trix would stay put. By this time, I'd moved into IT, via my father's firm, and we decided to go with the job I found here in Salisbury – not least because Manju has family round here.

Those couple of years were not without incident. Trix got pregnant by some drifter and had an abortion. There were some rumbling of a social services investigation into him living in the same house as the children – but I could never learn the details, because I was not 'directly' involved in the case. I was just paying support as determined by the CSA for both children (something I continued to do until their abduction). I was just buying their school uniforms and finding fees for nurseries and music lessons. I just made sure that the fridge was stocked every time I visited. But I wasn't 'involved'. Anyway, a year later, she miscarried the baby of another boyfriend. They were on the way to the airport for a holiday, so they buried it by the side of the road, with Sunil watching.

Amazingly, throughout this period, he continued to get good reports, though there were concerns about his social skills. In July 2000, Trix tried to take him out for 'home education' – supposedly because he wanted it – but I managed to avert it, with the help of my mother in law. Clearly Sunil had problems integrating at the school – his behaviour continued to deteriorate – but being at home with Trix was a worse alternative. Meanwhile, Anoushka took to school like the proverbial fish to water. She was top of the form, involved in all the after-hours clubs and activities.

By 2001, I was resigned to the idea that Trix was going to do whatever she wanted with Sunil. (She was talking about 'home education' again.) But I felt really anxious that

she might put Anoushka's happiness at risk – all the more when she started hassling me to have my passport altered, so that she could get the kids passports of their own. In retrospect, I think she was concocting a plan. When she did leave the country in July 2002, one reason she gave was that a local weirdo was stalking her. But a year before, she'd already started on that story. He'd slashed her tyres, but he'd also caused trouble for other people in the street – and anyway, a mutual friend of ours had warned him off.

In the summer of 2001, Trix took Sunil out of school. And over the next year, things really started to unravel. In March 2002, my family were having a special gathering for my grandfather's 85th birthday, and I'd arranged to take both children. But that weekend, when I arrived, Sunil said he wasn't coming. Of course, I got no support from Trix. So, to show how I felt, I confiscated a Game Boy I had 'lent' him. I said something like, 'Well you're not going to spend the weekend playing games on this. You can have it back next time I see you.'

Trix and I talked about the incident later, but her attitude was: 'Sort it out between you. He thinks you love Nush more than him – and he's cross about the Game Boy.' After that, despite my best efforts, Sunil never visited my new family again. Worse, my contact with Anoushka – and her stability – began to crumble under Trix's influence; and Trix's mother, Edith, who had kept some kind of minimal control over her before, had a kind of brainstorm. Her

husband had left her a few years before, and she'd married a guy who didn't want to get sucked into our problems. Edith now started taking Trix's side — with the eventual result that her second husband also left her, in disgust.

Anyway, fast forward to July 2002, and this is the situation. After years of really close relations with my first two children — seeing them every other weekend and half the holidays — things are suddenly falling apart. Trix has threatened to sell her house, and to go travelling in South America (though nothing has come of these plans except huge amounts of anxiety for me). And while Trix has been telling them to conceal the truth, Sunil and Anoushka have been taken out of school without consulting me.

By this time, Trix is refusing to talk to me at all. Sunil is difficult on the phone and insulting by email (though he soon drops that attitude when I see him). Anoushka is my only real point of contact and, on the occasions that we can organise pick-ups, we have to meet at the house of a friend of hers in Hove. When I learn that I can't take the kids on holiday to Scotland in August, as it conflicts with plans made later by Trix and Edith, I become seriously alarmed. I decide that, if I can't get satisfactory contact arrangements for the children and reasonable communication with Trix, I'll take legal advice.

Well, I phoned Brighton over and over, I got 'call waiting', I left messages, but there was no reply. I knew they were in, because Sunil was on my AOL 'buddy' list, so I

could see him signing on and off on his computer. On 9 July, I emailed him, asking if he wanted to come with Nush and me on a camping weekend – and could he tell Nush to get in touch. In response, I got a non-committal message from her, with a PS from Sunil, saying that he only wanted email contact from now on. That night, I emailed Trix, setting out my concerns and my intention to reluctantly seek legal advice if we couldn't resolve things.

I don't think that was the wrong thing to do. Unbeknown to me, Trix was already organising to sneak away. The next day, she sent me back an email, saying she wanted no further communication, nor discussion of the children's upbringing. Nor had she decided on the destination of their August 'holiday'. She called me a bully and a control freak, accused me of harassment and signed off: 'Enough said. Forever.'

Over the next fortnight, the children put off any plans I'd made with them, and I consulted a solicitor friend. He helped me to fill in the forms for the local court, and in early August I filed for a contact order and a review of Anoushka's education. (It was too late for Sunil.) The hearing was due in mid-September, and Trix had been given due notice. In late July, she even got Sunil to ring and say, 'Stop taking mummy to court about Nush's education.' But she didn't show. So the judge ordered another hearing, with statements from both sides and a CAFCASS report.

That night I rang Brighton – hoping to find out what Trix

was up to – and when I heard a different woman's voice on the answering machine, I guess I knew in my heart. I drove straight down there, but no one was in. I looked through the windows, and couldn't see any of the kids' usual mess. I peered through the letterbox and saw mail in the name of a woman I didn't know. So I went to see our mutual friend, and he told me that, the moment Trix had received a court summons, she'd packed up and let the house. He made some calls around town for me – and when Trix's tenant got back, we asked her for more information – but all we could discover was that Trix had been 'freaked out by the stalker and wouldn't be back'. I called my mum, we both called Edith, but whatever she knew, she wasn't letting on. I walked along the beach for hours that night, holding on to the unopened letters for my kids that had been returned to me by Trix's tenant.

Oh God, it went on, and I'm having to leave out so many ways in which I was provoked or hurt. Anyway, a couple of weeks later, I hired a solicitor who quoted me £300, and we got an order on Trix to disclose the kids' whereabouts. (That was only possible because I had parental responsibility for Sunil; in those days, your name on the birth certificate didn't guarantee it.) Now, although the order couldn't be served on her – because we didn't know where she was – it did mean the Child Abduction Unit could start a search in any country that was a signatory to the Hague Convention. The solicitor tried to charge me £800, and

the contact hearing was postponed. I joined Families Need Fathers, and started boxes for the kids in their room upstairs. It's still full of their things, from a few years ago.

But back to the case. In the end, I spent 18 months not knowing where on the face of the earth my children were, and I had no communication with them. It was a terrible time for the whole family. But with Interpol's help and veiled threats to Edith, Trix was eventually traced to Italy in December 2003. There, she was summonsed by the state prosecutor to attend a local Hague Convention hearing in February, but her solicitor managed to delay it on technicalities until April. In Britain, I was dealing with the Lord Chancellor's office – which was, I have to say, pretty useless.

Since it was such a black and white case of abduction – and also the state of Italy versus Trix – I didn't know if I needed to make a statement giving any background. I asked the Chancellor's office, and they couldn't give me an answer. So to be on the safe side, I took a couple of weeks off work and prepared a presentation. It's just as well – in one way – because about ten days before the hearing was first scheduled, I received a visit from an Italian prosecutor. Hire a Roman lawyer, he said. Since this was a Hague Convention issue, I asked about legal aid, but it wasn't available, so it cost me about £4000 in the end. And Italian lawyers are no better than British ones.

The case itself was fairly straightforward. The prosecutor made a five-minute statement, then my solicitor concentrated on aspects of my presentation that particularly applied to the Convention. Her solicitor replied to both, spouting a load of nonsense, but the judge had Trix's number. Four weeks later, we had our ruling: the kids should be returned to Britain within ten days, and stay here until the postponed contact hearing was held.

Trix tried manipulate me. And she definitely made things worse for the kids, which just made them blame me more. But at least it meant that I got to talk to them for the first time in over a year. As the deadline approached, Trix suddenly phoned with a deal. She didn't want to be dragged through 'the system', she said. If I could just be 'cool' and drop proceedings, she'd make sure that I could see the kids – so long as Manju wasn't involved. I didn't say anything, but I did take legal advice the next day – and was told in no uncertain terms not to co-operate.

That evening, I phoned back and asked to speak to the kids. Amazingly, Trix agreed. (I guess she'd primed them about the new deal.) What they said was worrying – Sunil was very hostile and sarcastic, and Nush claimed she couldn't remember me, let alone the rest of my family – but it was still great just to hear their voices. However, when Trix came back on the line and I told her 'no deal', she went nuts. She swore that, for as long as she lived, she'd do everything possible to stop our children seeing me.

She started by making the kids' homecoming difficult. She said she couldn't accompany them, claiming she feared her mythical stalker. And even though I was buying the tickets, she'd fixed it so that the children refused to see me. I had to pay extra for a 'universal aunt', who took them from Brindisi to Gatwick. It was mid-June – two weeks later than ordered – and they stayed with Edith until mid-August, when we went back to court. What a nerve-racking time that was. I discovered that Trix's mother had bought a house for them both in Italy; and since the order had been technically honoured, there was nothing to stop them taking off again.

In fact, Trix turned up at court – with a legal team. I was representing myself – and I was fairly disappointed. The judge confirmed that I had parental responsibility for Nush as well as Sunil. He also allowed the children's return to Italy, and made various directions: a minimum of indirect contact to be started immediately; schooling (at home or otherwise) to be full-time and not interrupted by travels; direct contact to be resumed if CAFCASS said it was okay. But directions aren't binding. When I asked for an order, he said that wouldn't be necessary, as he could see Trix nodding in agreement!

In theory, Trix and I then arranged for me to ring the kids every Sunday, at 10am their time. But I only called once. Sunil said, 'We're only talking to you because the judge forced mummy to say yes.' Anoushka joined in: 'We

hate you and all your family.' And, well, you know the rest. In September, Guy from CAFCASS came to observe me with the children, and didn't feel he could recommend direct contact. In November, we had the final hearing. And now I have to face the fact that I'll never see the children again. I've sent them Christmas cards and presents, money, letters, emails – but, as I expected, there's been no response. My mother tried to get some news from Trix's mother, but was told that she doesn't want to talk at the moment.

People try to comfort me by saying that every step I took was right. But I still can't agree with the court that what's happening will be right for the children. The emotional abuse of their abduction abroad will leave lifelong wounds on them – and like any abused child, they'll hide their pain. It's not until it comes out that we'll learn how much they were hurting – and then it'll be too late.

10. PAT

'Losing his daughter didn't just destroy our son; it
cast a shadow over our whole family.'

5 February 2005

*A small man still sprightly in his seventies, Pat is a member of
Fathers 4 Justice, but limits his activities to offering support outside court, in cases that are high profile among excluded fathers,
and to attending legal demonstrations.*

*In this, he has the full backing of his wife Freda, septuagenari-
an mother of four and grandmother to six more (including one
'step'). And as soon as you enter their lived-in Fifties villa — set
back from a main road in north Oxford — it's clear that the family is at the centre of their lives. The wallpaper is almost obscured by
pictures of their brood at every age, among them their eldest son
Kieran (tall, crop-headed, bespectacled), his petite Canadian ex-
wife Kelly and the couple's ten-year-old daughter Ruth.*

Kindly, conservative, churchgoing, the couple spent their working lives in middle management. Now both are deeply saddened to have their retirements blighted by the fallout from the failed marriage of Kieran, 41, to Kelly, 38. They have watched their son suffer a breakdown since losing contact with Ruth; and having been a major part of their only granddaughter's life for several years, they miss her terribly, too.

Pat and Freda have no legal right to any contact with Ruth, and Kieran's is now minimal. (In 18 months, it has amounted to a few phone calls to Ruth, three photographs of her, two Christmas cards from her, and Kelly's emailed acknowledgments of gifts.) Ruth herself has been released from UK jurisdiction and taken to Canada, where she now lives with Kelly and grandmother Ronnie. Pat tries his hardest not to blame his former in-laws, and seems more astounded than angry. But he says the strain has told less on him than on Freda, who sits anxiously on the sofa beside him...

***

Kieran's in Africa at the moment, and communications have been sporadic recently, so I can't really check dates and details, and I'm a bit hazy about them. Also, my interpretation of things may be different from his. But as I see it, he was an extremely good father, it's a terrible world that can let this happen to him, and it's come about because Kelly can't admit to herself that she is more to blame than him for the failure of their marriage. Partly, that was because she

was reverting to type, which I can understand, even if I don't approve. (You see, her parents were very well off; and after they divorced when she was 12, she was raised by her mother, who was a real go-getter.) But partly, it was because of her infidelity – and she should face up to that.

Kelly came to Britain on a year out from a university degree – which she must have started quite late – and she stayed for nine. But now it's like she thinks all those nine years were her wild times and she can just put them behind her. I suppose she doesn't want to be reminded of how she behaved. But also, I don't think she wants the bother. You know, she wants a new life, not to be tied down by contact arrangements every other weekend, or to fit in with Ruth when she wants to see her English relations. The tragedy is that, to achieve her goal, Kelly appears to have been turning Ruth against Kieran – against all of us – and she's so special to us.

For instance, on Christmas Day 2003, there were lots of family here, and we were all excited because Kieran had made an e-mail arrangement with Kelly to ring Ruth at 6 in the evening. When Kelly put her on, you could register the shock in his face. 'Hello, Roo,' he said. Then, a couple of seconds later: 'Let me put you on to your uncle Francis, then.' Now Francis is Freda's brother, and he's everyone's favourite. He'd do anything for anyone, and he and Ruth were always very close. And do you know what she said to him? The same as she'd said to Kieran: 'I hate you.' Well,

Francis passed her on to our daughter Bernie, and Bernie passed her on to her son Ben – who'd been one of Ruth's best friends – and to every one of them she said the same thing: 'I hate you. I hate you.' But that isn't the behaviour of a normal, happy child.

When Kieran had stopped crying, he lay down on this sofa and fell asleep. I think he was completely exhausted by the stress. And shortly after that, he left his job at the nursing home and found one at a garden centre. It was good for his depression to be outside more, and working with his hands. But the main reason was that he felt so isolated. Many of the helpers at Evergreens were temporary – often they couldn't speak English – so he couldn't really look to them for sympathy. And he was finding it too much to care for the old folk, who were mainly senile. He needed help as much as them.

Actually, it was through the caring profession that he met Kelly, in 1992. He'd left school at 16, drifted through various jobs before training as a carer, and ended up with his own flat and a job at Evergreens, a nursing home five miles north of here. Now Kelly, as I say, was over on a sort of gap year, working for her keep. Her mother was a hospital administrator (who also ran an internet footwear company) so I suppose she naturally looked for health-sector jobs. And that's how she came to be an orderly at Evergreens.

Well, they started going out together, and fell in love.

Kelly decided to put her degree on hold, trained as a carer and found a job at another nursing home. And because they both shared a love of the countryside, they rented a flat together, about another five miles north. It was part of a huge, tumbledown livery stable that was being converted, and the residents did quite a lot of things communally – parties and barbecues, for instance. Among the friends they made there was a neighbour called Martin.

By the end of 1993, Kelly was pregnant, and they got married. In May 1994, Ruth was born and Grandma Ronnie came over for the christening. It was the first of several visits – which we later returned – and we all got on very well. One thing I remember, though. The first time Ronnie visited the stables, she said, 'You know what I'd do with this place? I'd put in a pool and a multi-gym and an organic restaurant.' I mean, that would have cost about five million. Where did she think Kieran could raise that kind of money? As it was, he got into terrible trouble with his credit cards, because Kelly was flying to Toronto two or three times a year when they were together, and he often went with her.

That wasn't their only problem. In their line, there's a lot of shift work, so one might be on mornings and the other on nights, or they'd both be on at the same time. And that's where we came in. We often say that, for the first years of her life, we were Ruth's real parents, because we had her two-thirds of the time, overnights included.

Normally, she was dropped off and picked up by her mum or dad, but we often had to do the driving ourselves. It wasn't ideal for them – perhaps it put a strain on their marriage – but we loved it. With so many grandsons, the only girl was always very precious to us. And she was such good fun, a real live wire.

Anyway, from the outside, they seemed happy enough. Kelly wasn't really a hands-on mum, but Kieran loved being a dad. He'd play shops and go swimming with Ruth. He'd help her to bake a cake, or look after the rabbits that he bought her. Over time, we noticed that Kelly was at home less and less – and we could sense that something wasn't quite right – but Kieran would just say she was working. In hindsight, he was probably hiding the truth from himself. But after they split in 1999, it all came out.

About three years after Ruth was born, one of their neighbours at the stables died. At the funeral, Kelly met a friend of Martin's called Robin, and in time started an affair with him. He was in his fifties then, very well heeled, and we've often wondered if she was looking for a father figure. Martin helped Robin and Kelly by making his flat available to them – but she pretended that she had just developed a very close friendship with Martin. She always seemed to be over at his place. Once, when we dropped Ruth on a Sunday, only Kieran was there. 'How's Kelly?' we asked. 'She's over at Martin's,' he said.

It appears things went from bad to worse – though all

we knew at the time was that they were rowing, because sometimes we would hear Kieran calling Kelly from our phone. Later, we learned all sorts of things: that Kelly had befriended a recently divorced woman, who probably put a lot of ideas into her head; that she had been going off on weekends without Kieran; that, eventually, she was openly seeing Robin. As it was, in late 1999, we were surprised when Kieran told us they were separating. He said: 'Dad, I've found a flat near Evergreens. Can you help me move some stuff?'

If he had his time again, of course, he would have stayed put. But he wasn't to know the unfairness of the system. He just wanted Ruth to have as much stability as possible – her home, her mum, the new place she'd got at school. Kelly seemed rooted in the area, she loved the countryside, and Robin lived nearby. With Kieran paying her rent and a sum set by the CSA, he never thought she'd move away, let alone emigrate.

I can't really remember the exact sequence of events after that. I know we still did a lot of babysitting, and that our sense of unease grew slowly. Once, when Freda and I went round, we found a young chap looking after Ruth, and we were concerned that we hadn't been asked. Another time, when we dropped by on chance, another chap who was doing the garden let us in; and although Kelly was upstairs, she wouldn't come down to see us, so we left after half an hour. But at first, the handovers went quite smoothly. Kieran saw Ruth here every other weekend and

half the holidays, and we shared all the driving with him.

Kelly was already making problems – cancelling dates because Ruth was supposedly ill, stopping her from ringing her cousins and so on – but her attitude didn't really harden until late 2000. That was when the divorce was going through, and she announced she was moving to the other side of Banbury. (She rented a house there, supposedly on her own, but we've since learned that Robin shared it some of the time.) It was also around then that she engineered a falling-out between Ronnie and us – until then, we'd kept in touch on the phone – and that Kieran discovered she'd pocketed all the rent money he'd been sending her. The lease was in his name, so he had to pay about a year's arrears in the end – on top of all those credit card debts. Kelly told him that, otherwise, he'd never see Ruth again.

When Kieran arranged mediation, Kelly missed the first appointment, refused to talk about anything but money at the second, and stormed out of the third. That's when she started being downright cruel. When Ruth's coat got torn, for instance, Kelly sent a note saying, 'Pay for it, or you don't see Ruth next fortnight.' She stopped Ruth doing overnights here, claiming she didn't like them – although Ruth used to love coming to play with Ben; sometimes we almost had to drag her to the car. And when Kieran sent a note and some presents to Ruth, he got a solicitor's letter back, claiming harassment.

He couldn't win. Kelly also used to withdraw contact if

Kieran disciplined Ruth. Once he said to me, 'How can I be a proper dad when I'm walking on eggshells the whole time?' And in January 2001, I remember, he broke down in tears. It had been three months since he'd seen Ruth. He'd been put off and messed around so that he didn't even have her over the Christmas holidays, and he'd had enough. He told us he'd been to some FNF meetings, and decided to take Kelly to court. Well, we were shocked. We had no idea about courts – we thought they were for criminals – but after I'd been to a few meetings with Kieran, I realised why fathers were driven to it.

It's so sad, and it's the same at F4J. You see these dads arriving, with their papers and their clipboards – all pre-pared for their court cases, looking forward to getting some justice – and you know they haven't got a snowflake's chance in hell. Of course, we didn't realise that then. But we soon discovered that, as grandparents, we had no say – even though Ruth had probably spent more time with us than both her parents. We weren't even allowed into the court-room to listen, and when a CAFCASS report was done, they refused to take our evidence. I mean, why call it 'fam-ily law' when it doesn't seem to recognise the extended family?

But back to Ruth. All Kieran wanted was for Kelly to stick by their deal, and he thought that the threat of legal action – or if necessary, a court order – would bring her to her senses. Her tactics in reply were to observe the letter of the agreement, but not the spirit, then use the courts to

mess him about. When Kieran was an hour late back from a trip to Devon with Ruth, Kelly claimed that it proved he couldn't be trusted. But when she was an hour late and he rang her to discover her whereabouts, she got onto the police and said he was harassing her. They came round and grilled him for two hours.

The hearings went on for over a year. Between Ruth's seventh birthday, when Kieran had her for an hour, and her eighth, when he went to joint-party with a friend of hers, he didn't see her at all. But I've lost count of how many times he was in court. You know, he'd turn up at one hearing, and it would be postponed for two months, and then he'd get another judge. Plus, all the time, he was being bombarded with letters from Kelly's solicitor. She had legal aid – she even had a barrister – but he was representing himself, some-times with the help of a 'McKenzie Friend'*.

In the end, the court confirmed the original contact arrangements – plus Kieran was allowed one phone call a week – but it all hinged on one point. Kelly said that she felt intimidated by Kieran at the handovers, so it was agreed between them, the CAFCASS officer and the judge that

* This term derives from a 1980s contact case in Australia, when a Mr McKenzie successfully appealed against a bar on him bringing an amateur, unpaid adviser into a family court. Britain has since followed Australia's lead, and now experienced members of such groups as FNF and F4J often act as McKenzie Friends to colleagues who are less well versed in legal matters. However, some judges here still find pretexts to bar them.

Freda and I would do all the driving. Now, that meant a diary commitment and two 30-mile trips every other weekend, but that wasn't what annoyed me. I couldn't believe that the same CAFCASS officer who'd decided our evidence was irrelevant could decide to make us the main plank of his strategy – and not consult us! It's the only time I lost my temper in the whole episode, and I'm afraid I tore quite a strip off him later, when I got him on the phone. To make it worse, when Kelly came out of the courtroom, she punched the air, as if she'd won a personal victory.

For the next year or so, Kelly kept to the timetable, but Ruth's attitude began to change. Every time I picked her up, it took longer for the ice to thaw. I got round that by putting a bag with some sweets or a toy in it on the back seat. She'd start off completely silent, but her curiosity always got the better of her, and once she opened the bag, she'd be chattering away as usual. She was the same with Kieran – only withdrawn at first – but he took it a lot worse than us.

The crisis came in May 2003, and we have to presume it was genuine. Ruth had been taken to Canada for Easter, and when they came back, Kelly was very ill with cardiac problems. She had a consultant's letter to prove it, and you could say she used that to engineer her return to Canada. You see, with Ronnie's job, Kelly could get immediate, world-class treatment in Toronto, but she'd be on the NHS here. Well, she had Kieran over a barrel. He couldn't

endanger her health by objecting – so she could go there for as long as it took. Well, we all went to wave Ruth off from Heathrow in May, which is when we first saw Robin; none of us knows if he and Kelly were – or are – still a couple.

Anyway, in June, Kelly struck. Kieran received a letter saying she wanted to start a new life and couldn't be tied down by him, so she wanted their agreement legally cancelled. As I recall, it was all a huge rush, sorted out on a speakerphone in a family courtroom; and it didn't help that, because Kieran's McKenzie wasn't around, he had to consult a solicitor. But she advised him – probably rightly – that the best he could hope for would be some postal and telephone contact, and an undertaking from Kelly that she wouldn't prevent Ruth from seeking further contact if that's what she wanted. So he agreed to those terms.

After that, Kieran went into serious decline. Although he was diagnosed with depression by his doctor, who gave him a sick note and a prescription, he never took the pills. Still, the rest, followed by the gardening job, helped him. And at first, so did joining F4J. Going on demos was a way for him to express his emotions. But listening to other members' stories stirred up such painful feelings that his state of mind was affected; so, about a year ago, he decided to keep away from the group meetings.

That's when he moved back in with us, and started saving up to travel. He left in July and should be back in a few weeks. I suppose, with all his hopes dashed, he just wanted

to get away for a while and come back to a new start. Also, he was worried about becoming obsessed by the whole issue. Actually, that's why he didn't want me to get involved with F4J. 'You'll become *too* involved,' he said, and he was right. But we've reacted differently. I've transferred the energy I once spent on my granddaughter into the group.

It's not that I'm still fighting for Kieran and Ruth. (Though Freda and I talk about her every day, we realise there's nothing more we can do.) It's just, in my case, I can't walk away from a social injustice that's happening on such a massive scale. If I can only offer moral support to other dads and granddads, I'm doing something. And I tell you, even if Ruth came back to England, and Kieran was her main carer, I'd still stay in F4J. There's a principle here. Each parent should have the child half the time. Now, in the real world, that couldn't work. But at least, under those conditions, there would be official recognition that fathers can be flexible in the best interests of the child.

Of course, there's always the issue of the extended family. You see, losing Ruth didn't just destroy Kieran; it cast a shadow over our whole family. And more important than that, it robbed Ruth of the happiness and security she might have got from growing up with Freda and me, and all her aunts and uncles and cousins. But if the law can't deal fairly with fathers, what hope has the rest of us got?

ACKNOWLEDGEMENTS

Many thanks to all the excluded fathers with whom I have had dealings – and particularly to the interviewees. Thanks, too, to everyone at Families Need Fathers, especially press officer Jim Parton and webmaster John Robertson. I am also indebted to Henrietta McMillan-Scott, the eminent solicitor in this field, for enlightening me on several aspects of family law – and to Chris Dawkins, for guiding me through international attitudes to 'move away'.

I'M A TEACHER
GET ME OUT OF HERE!
Francis Gilbert

At last, here it is. The book that tells you the unvarnished truth about teaching. By turns hilarious, sobering, and downright horrifying, I'm a Teacher, Get me Out of Here! contains the sort of information that you won't find in any school prospectus, government advert or Hollywood film.

Francis Gilbert candidly describes the remarkable way in which he was trained to be a teacher, his terrifying first lesson and his even more frightening experiences in his first job at Truss comprehensive, one of the worst schools in the country. Follow him on his rollercoaster journey through the world that is the English education system; encounter thuggish and charming children, terrible and brilliant teachers; learn about the sinister effects of school inspectors and the teacher's disease of 'controloholism'. Spy on what really goes on behind the closed doors of inner-city schools.

> "A fascinating and finely observed account of
> an inner city school."
> Peter Ackroyd

1-904977-02-2

How to be a Bad Birdwatcher
To the greater glory of life
Simon Barnes
1-904095-95-X

Look out of the window.
See a bird.
Enjoy it.
Congratulations. You are now a bad birdwatcher.

Anyone who has ever gazed up at the sky or stared out of the window knows something about birds. In this funny, inspiring, eye-opening book, Simon Barnes paints a riveting picture of how bird-watching has framed his life and can help us all to a better understanding of our place on this planet.

How to be a bad birdwatcher shows why birdwatching is not the preserve of twitchers, but one of the simplest, cheapest and most rewarding pastimes around.

"An ode to the wild world outside the kitchen window"
Daily Telegraph

GOING BUDDHIST
Panic and emptiness, the Buddha and me
Peter J Conradi

About twenty years ago, Peter Conradi's life hit the bumpers, and he began suffering from terrifying panic attacks. This book is his account of the new life-journey he embarked on back then, when, with the help of his friend and mentor Iris Murdoch, he began to explore Buddhism.

Each year in the UK, as Conradi describes, 22 million prescriptions are written for tranquillisers, and yet Buddhism can provide a third way. During meditation one's heart rate slows down and brain rhythms become calmer.

Full of wise comedy, this is a self-help book for cynics, in which Conradi seeks to explain the beauty of Buddhism, a religion now more relevant than ever to Westerners, perishing from the nihilism of the age.

"...a short, sweet and enchanting book... Conradi's account of his epiphany is an inspiration."
Mick Brown, DAILY TELEGRAPH

1-904977-01-4

A father of one, Tim Willis has previously written the biography of a rock'n'roll recluse. *Madcap: The Half-Life of Syd Barrett, Pink Floyd's Lost Genius* is also published by Short Books.

TORN APART